Anthony Hope

The Chronicles of Count Antonio

Anthony Hope

The Chronicles of Count Antonio

ISBN/EAN: 9783743349995

Manufactured in Europe, USA, Canada, Australia, Japa

Cover: Foto ©ninafisch / pixelio.de

Manufactured and distributed by brebook publishing software (www.brebook.com)

Anthony Hope

The Chronicles of Count Antonio

THE LIBRARY
OF
THE UNIVERSITY
OF CALIFORNIA
LOS ANGELES

THE
CHRONICLES OF COUNT ANTONIO

THE CHRONICLES OF COUNT ANTONIO

BY
ANTHONY HOPE
AUTHOR OF THE PRISONER OF ZENDA, ETC.

WITH PHOTOGRAVURE FRONTISPIECE BY S. W. VAN SCHAICK

NEW YORK
D. APPLETON AND COMPANY
1895

COPYRIGHT, 1895,
BY ANTHONY HOPE.

COPYRIGHT, 1895,
BY D. APPLETON AND COMPANY.

TO THE
HONOURABLE SIR HENRY HAWKINS.

MY DEAR SIR HENRY:

It gives me very great pleasure to be allowed to dedicate this book to you. I hope you will accept it as a token of thanks for much kindness, of your former Marshal's pleasant memory of his service, and of sincere respect for a clear-sighted, firm, and compassionate Judge.

Your affectionate cousin,

A. H. H.

London, August, 1895.

CONTENTS.

CHAPTER	PAGE
I.—How Count Antonio took to the Hills . .	1
II.—Count Antonio and the Traitor Prince .	39
III.—Count Antonio and the Prince of Mantivoglia.	71
IV.—Count Antonio and the Wizard's Drug . .	116
V.—Count Antonio and the Sacred Bones . .	158
VI.—Count Antonio and the Hermit of the Vault .	202
VII.—Count Antonio and the Lady of Rilano . .	245
VIII.—The Manner of Count Antonio's Return . .	290

THE CHRONICLES OF COUNT ANTONIO.

CHAPTER I.

HOW COUNT ANTONIO TOOK TO THE HILLS.

COUNTLESS are the stories told of the sayings that Count Antonio spoke and of the deeds that he did when he dwelt an outlaw in the hills. For tales and legends gather round his name thick as the berries hang on a bush, and with the passage of every succeeding year it grows harder to discern where truth lies and where the love of wonder, working together with the sway of a great man's memory, has wrought the embroidery of its fancy on the plain robe of fact. Yet, amid all that is of uncertain knowledge and so must rest, this much at least should be known and remembered for the honour of a noble family, how it fell out that Count Antonio, a man of high lineage, forsook the service of his Prince, disdained the obligation of his rank, set law at naught, and did what seemed indeed in his own eyes to be good but was held by many to be nothing other than the work of a rebel and a brigand. Yet, although it is by these names that men often speak of him, they love his memory; and I also, Ambrose the Franciscan, having gathered diligently all that I could come by in the archives of the city or from the lips of aged folk, have learned to love it in some sort. Thus I am minded to write, before the time that I must carry what I know with me to the grave, the full and whole truth concerning Antonio's flight from the city and the Court, seeking in my heart, as I write, excuse for him, and finding in the record, if little else, yet a tale that lovers must read in pride and sorrow, and, if this be not too high a hope, that princes may study for profit and for warning.

Now it was in the tenth year of the reign of Duke Valentine over the city of Firmola, its territories and dependent towns, that Count Antonio of Monte Velluto—having with him a youthful cousin of his, whom he loved greatly, and whom, by reason of his small stature and of a boyish gaiety he had, men called Tommasino—came from his own house on the hill that fronts the great gate of the city, to the palace of the Duke, with intent to ask His Highness's sanction for his marriage with the Lady Lucia. This lady, being then seventeen years of age, loved Antonio, and he her, and troth had been privily plighted between them for many months; and such was the strength and power of the love they bore the one to the other, that even to this day the old mock at young lovers who show themselves overfond, crying, "'Tis Lucia and Antonio!"

But since the Lady Lucia was an orphan, Antonio came now to the Duke, who enjoyed wardship over her, and setting out his passion and how that his estate was sufficient and his family such as the Duke knew, prayed leave of His Highness to wed her. But the Duke, a crafty and subtle prince, knowing Antonio's temper and the favour in which he was held by the people, counted not to augment his state and revenues by the gift of a bride so richly dowered, but chose rather to give her to a favourite of his, a man in whose devotion he could surely trust and whose disposition was to serve his master in all things fair and foul, open or secret. Such an one the Duke found in the Lord Robert de Beauregard, a gentleman of Provence, who had quitted his own country, having been drawn into some tumult there, and, having taken service with the Duke, had risen to a great place in his esteem and confidence. Therefore, when Antonio preferred his request, the Duke, with many a courteous regretful phrase, made him aware that the lady stood promised to Robert by the irrevocable sanctity of his princely pledge.

"So forget, I pray you, my good cousin Antonio," said he, "forget, as young men lightly can, this desire of yours, and it shall be my charge to find you a bride full as fair as the Lady Lucia."

But Antonio's face went red from brow to chin, as he answered: "My gracious lord, I love the lady, and she me, and neither can wed another. As for my Lord Robert, your Highness knows well that she loves him not."

"A girl's love!" smiled the Duke. "A girl's

love! It rains and shines, and shines and rains, Antonio."

"It has shone on me since she knew a man when she looked on him," said Antonio.

And Tommasino, who stood by, recking as little of the Duke as of the Duke's deerhound which he was patting the while, broke in, saying carelessly, "And this Robert, my lord, is not the man for a pretty girl to love. He is a sour fellow."

"I thank you for your counsel, my lord Tommasino," smiled the Duke. "Yet I love him." Whereat Tommasino lifted his brows and patted the hound again. "It is enough," added the Duke. "I have promised, Antonio. It is enough."

"Yes, it is enough," said Antonio; and he and Tommasino, having bowed low, withdrew from the presence of the Duke. But when he got clear outside of the Duke's cabinet, Antonio laid his hand on Tommasino's shoulder, saying, "It is not well that Robert have her."

"It is mighty ill," said Tommasino.

And then they walked in silence to the city

gate, and, in silence still, climbed the rugged hill where Antonio's house stood.

But the Duke sent for Robert de Beauregard into his cabinet and said to him: "If you be wise, friend Robert, little grass shall grow under your feet this side your marriage. This Antonio says not much; but I have known him outrun his tongue with deeds."

"If the lady were as eager as I, the matter would not halt," said Robert with a laugh. "But she weeps and spits fire at me, and cries for Antonio."

"She will be cured after the wedding," said the Duke. "But see that she be well guarded, Robert; let a company of your men watch her. I have known the bride to be missing on a marriage day ere now."

"If he can touch her, he may wed her," cried Robert. "The pikemen are close about her house, and she can neither go in nor come forth without their knowledge."

"It is well," said the Duke. "Yet delay not. They are stubborn men, these Counts of Monte Velluto."

Now had the Lady Lucia been of a spirit as haughty as her lover's, it may be that she would have refused to wed Robert de Beauregard. But she was afraid. When Antonio was with her, she had clung to him, and he loved her the more for her timidity. With him gone and forbidden to come near her, she dared not resist the Duke's will nor brave his displeasure; so that a week before the day which the Duke had appointed for the wedding, she sent to Antonio, bidding him abandon a hope that was vain and set himself to forget a most unhappy lady.

"Robert shall not have her," said Antonio, putting the letter in his belt.

"Then the time is short," said Tommasino.

They were walking together on the terrace before Antonio's house, whence they looked on the city across the river. Antonio cast his eye on the river and on the wall of the Duke's garden that ran along it; fair trees, shrubs, and flowers lined the top of the wall, and the water gleamed in the sunshine.

"It is strange," said Antonio, musing, "that one maiden can darken for a man all the world that God lights with his sun. Yet since so it is, Tommasino, a man can be but a man; and being a man, he is a poor man, if he stand by while another takes his love."

"And that other a stranger, and, as I swear, a cut-throat," added Tommasino.

When they had dined and evening began to come on, Antonio made his servants saddle the best horses in his stable—though, indeed, the choice was small, for Antonio was not rich as a man of his rank counts riches—and the two rode down the hill towards the city. But, as they went, Antonio turned once and again in his saddle and gazed long at the old gray house, the round tower, and the narrow gate.

"Why look behind, and not forward?" asked Tommasino.

"Because there is a foreboding in me," answered Antonio, "that it will be long before that gate again I pass through. Were there a hope of persuading you, Tommasino, I would bid you turn back, and leave me to go alone on this errand."

"Keep your breath against when you have to

run," laughed Tommasino, pricking his horse and tossing his hair, dark as Antonio's was fair, back from his neck.

Across the bridge they rode and through the gates, and having traversed the great square, came to the door of Lucia's house, where it rose fronting the Duke's palace. Here Antonio dismounted, giving his bridle into Tommasino's hand, and bade the servants carry his name to the Lady Lucia. A stir arose among them and much whispering, till an old man, head of the servingmen, came forward, saying: "Pardon, my lord, but we are commanded not to admit you to the Lady Lucia;" and he waved his hand towards the inner part of the porch, where Antonio saw a dozen or more pikemen of the Duke's Guard drawn across the passage to the house; and their pikes flashed in the rays of the setting sun as they levelled them in front of their rank.

Some of the townsmen and apprentice lads, stout fellows, each with a staff, had gathered now around Antonio, whom they loved for his feats of strength and his liberal gifts to the poor, and, understanding what was afoot, one came to him, saying: "There are some, my lord, who would enter with you if you are set on entering," and the fellow's eyes sparkled; for there was a great enmity in the town against the pikemen, and a lusty youth with a stick in his hand is never loth to find a use for it.

For a moment Count Antonio hesitated; for they flocked closer to him, and Tommasino threw him a glance of appeal and touched the hilt of his sword. But he would not that the blood of men who were themselves loved by mothers, wives, and maids, should be shed in his quarrel, and he raised his hand, bidding them be still.

"I have no quarrel with the pikeman," said he, "and we must not fight against His Highness's servants."

The faces of the townsmen grew long in disappointment. Tommasino alone laughed low, recognising in Antonio's gentleness the lull that heralds a storm. The Count was never more dangerous than when he praised submission.

"But," continued Antonio, "I would fain see the Lady Lucia." And with this he stepped inside the porch, signing to Tommasino to stay where he was; but the lad would not, and, leaping down, ran to his kinsman and stood shoulder to shoulder with him.

Thus they stood facing the line of pikemen, when suddenly the opposing rank opened and Robert de Beauregard himself came through. Starting slightly on sight of Antonio, he yet bowed courteously, baring his head, and Antonio, with Tommasino, did the like.

"What is your desire, my lord?" asked Robert.

"I have naught to ask of you," answered Antonio, and he took a step forward. Robert's hand flew to his sword, and in a moment they would have fought. But now another figure came forward with uplifted hand. It was the Duke himself, and he looked on Antonio with his dark smile, and Antonio flushed red.

"You seek me, Antonio?" asked the Duke.

"I seek not your Highness, but my plighted wife," said Antonio.

Duke Valentine smiled still. Coming to Antonio, he passed his arm through his, and said in most friendly fashion: "Come with me to my house, and we will talk of this;" and Antonio, caught fast in the choice between obedience and open revolt, went frowning across the square, the Duke's arm through his, Robert on the Duke's other side, and, behind, Tommasino with the horses. But as they went, a sudden cry came from the house they left, and a girl's face showed for an instant, tear-stained and pallid, at an open window. A shiver ran through Antonio; but the Duke pressing his arm, he went still in silence.

At the door of the palace, a lackey took the horses from Tommasino, and the four passed through the great hall and through the Duke's cabinet beyond and into the garden; there the Duke sat down under the wall of the garden, near by the fish-pond, and turning suddenly on Antonio, spoke to him fiercely; "Men have died at my hands for less," said he.

"Then for each of such shall you answer to God," retorted Antonio, not less hotly.

"You scout my commands in the face of all the city," said the Duke in low stern tones.

"Now, by Heaven, if you seek to see the girl again, I will hang you from the tower of the gate. So be warned—now—once: there shall be no second warning."

He ceased, and sat with angry eyes on Antonio; and Robert, who stood by his master, glared as fierce. But Antonio was silent for a while, and rested his arm on Tommasino's shoulder.

"My fathers have served and fought for your fathers," said he at last. "What has this gentleman done for the Duchy?"

Then Robert spoke suddenly and scornfully: "This he is ready to do, to punish an insolent knave that braves His Highness's will."

Antonio seemed not to hear him, for he did not move but stood with eyes bent on the Duke's face, looking whether his appeal should reach its mark. But Tommasino heard; yet never a word spoke Tommasino either, but he drew off the heavy riding-glove from his left hand, and it hung dangling in the fingers of his right, and he looked at the glove and at Robert and at the glove again.

"I would his Highness were not here," said Tommasino to Robert with a smile.

"Hold your peace, boy," said Robert, "or the Duke will have you whipped."

Youth loves not to be taunted with its blessed state. "I have no more to say," cried Tommasino; and without more, caring naught now for the presence of the Duke, he flung his heavy glove full in Robert's face, and, starting back a pace, drew his sword. Then Antonio knew that the die was cast, for Tommasino would gain no mercy, having insulted the Duke's favourite and drawn his sword in the Duke's palace; and he also drew out his sword, and the pair stood facing the Duke and Robert de Beauregard. It was but for an instant that they stood thus; then Robert, who did not lack courage to resent a blow, unsheathed and rushed at the boy. Antonio left his cousin to defend himself, and, bowing low to the Duke, set his sword at the Duke's breast, before the Duke could so much as rise from his seat.

"I would not touch your Highness," said he, "but these gentlemen must not be interrupted."

"You take me at a disadvantage," cried the Duke.

"If you will swear not to summon your guard, I will sheath my sword, my lord; or, if you will honour me by crossing yours on mine, you shall draw yours."

The place where they sat was hidden from the palace windows, yet the Duke trusted that the sound of the clashing steel would bring aid; therefore, not desiring to fight with Antonio (for Duke Valentine loved to scheme rather than to strike), he sat still, answering nothing. And now Tommasino and Robert were engaged, Robert attacking furiously and Tommasino parrying him as coolly as though they fenced for pastime in the school. It was Tommasino's fault to think of naught but the moment and he did not remember that every second might bring the guard upon them. And Antonio would not call it to his mind, but he said to the Duke: "The boy will kill him, sir. He is a finer swordsman than I, and marvellously active."

Then the Duke, having been pondering on his course, and knowing Antonio—sitting there with the Count's sword against his breast—did by calculation what many a man braver in fight had not dared to do. There was in truth a courage in it, for all that it was born of shrewdness. For, thus with the sword on his heart, fixing a calm glance on Antonio, he cried as loudly as he could, "Help, help, treason!"

Antonio drew back his arm for the stroke; and the Duke sat still; then, swift as thought, Antonio laughed, bowed to Duke Valentine and, turning, rushed between the fighters, striking up their swords. In amazement they stood for a moment: Antonio drove his sword into its sheath, and, while Robert was yet astounded, he rushed on him, caught him by the waist, and, putting forth his strength, flung him clear and far into the fish-pond. Then seizing Tommasino by the arm he started with him at a run for the great hall. The Duke rose, crying loudly, "Treason, treason!" But Antonio cried "Treason, treason," yet louder than the Duke; and presently Tommasino, who had frowned at his pastime being interrupted, fell a-laughing, and between the laughs cried "Treason, treason!" with Antonio.

And at the entrance of the hall they met a dozen pikemen running; and Antonio, pointing over his shoulder, called in tones of horror, "Treason, treason!" And Tommasino cried, "The Duke! Help the Duke!" So that they passed untouched through the pikemen, who hesitated an instant in bewilderment but then swept on; for they heard the Duke's own voice crying still "Treason, treason!" And through the hall and out to the portico passed the cousins, echoing their cries of "Treason!" And every man they met went whither they pointed; and when they leapt on their horses, the very lackey that had held them dropped the bridles with hasty speed and ran into the palace, crying "Treason!" Then Antonio, Tommasino ever following, and both yet crying "Treason!" dashed across the square; and on the way they met the pikemen who guarded the Lady Lucia, and the townsmen who were mocking and snarling at the pikemen; and to pikemen and townsmen alike they cried (though Tommasino hardly could speak now for laughter and lack of breath), "Treason, treason!" And all to whom they cried flocked to the palace, crying in their turn, "Treason, treason!" so that people ran out of every house in the neighbourhood and hurried to the palace, crying "Treason!" and every one asking his neighbour what the treason was. And thus, by the time in which a man might count a hundred, a crowd was pushing and pressing and striving round the gate of the palace, and the cousins were alone on the other side of the great square.

"Now thanks be to God for that idea!" gasped Tommasino.

But Antonio gave not thanks till his meal was ended. Raising his voice as he halted his horse before the Lady Lucia's house, he called loudly, no longer "Treason!" but "Lucia!" And she, knowing his voice, looked out again from the window; but some hand plucked her away as soon as she had but looked. Then Antonio leapt from his horse with an oath and ran to the door, and finding it unguarded, he rushed in, leaving Tommasino seated on one horse and holding the other, with one eye on Lucia's house and the other on the palace, praying that, by the favour of Heaven, Antonio might come out again before the crowd round the Duke's gates discovered why it was, to a man, crying "Treason!"

But in the palace of the Duke there was great confusion. For the pikemen, finding Robert de Beauregard scrambling out of the fish-pond with a drawn sword in his hand, and His Highness crying "Treason!" with the best of them, must have it that the traitor was none other than Robert himself, and in their dutiful zeal they came nigh to making an end of him then and there, before the Duke could gain silence enough to render his account of the affair audible. And when the first pikemen were informed, there came others; and these others, finding the first thronging round the Duke and Robert, cried out on them for the traitors, and were on the point of engaging them; and when they also had been with difficulty convinced, and the two parties, with His Highness and Robert, turned to the pursuit of the cousins, they found the whole of the great hall utterly blocked by a concourse of the townsmen, delighted beyond measure at the chance of an affray with the hated pikemen, who, they conceived, must beyond doubt be the wicked traitors that had risen in arms against the Duke's life and throne. Narrowly indeed was a great battle in the hall averted by the Duke himself, who leapt upon a high seat and spoke long and earnestly to the people, persuading them that not the pikemen, but Antonio and Tommasino, were the traitors; which the townsmen found hard to believe, in part because they wished not to believe ill of Antonio, and more inasmuch as every man there knew—and the women and children also—that Antonio and Tommasino, and none else of all the city had raised the alarm. But some hearkened at last; and with these and a solid wedge of the pikemen, the Duke and Robert, with much ado, thrust their way through the crowd and won access to the door of the palace.

In what time a thousand men may be convinced, you may hope to turn one woman's mind, and at the instant that the Duke gained the square with his friends and his guards, Count Antonio had prevailed on the Lady Lucia to brave His Highness's wrath. It is true that he had met with some resistance from the steward, who was in Robert's pay, and had tarried to buffet the fellow into obedience; and with more from an old governess, who, since she could not be buffeted, had perforce to be locked in a cupboard; yet the better part of the time had to be spent in imploring Lucia herself. At last, with many fears and some tears, she had yielded, and it was with glad eyes that Tommasino saw the Count come forth from the door carrying Lucia on his arm; and others saw him also; for a great shout came from the Duke's party across the square, and the pikemen set out at a run with Robert himself at their head. Yet so soon as they were started, Antonio also, bearing Lucia in his arms, had reached where Tommasino was with the horses, and an instant later he was mounted and cried, "To the gate!" and he struck in his spurs, and his horse bounded forward, Tommasino following. No more than a hundred yards lay between them and the gate of the city, and before the pikemen could bar their path they had reached the gate. The gatewardens were in the act of shutting it, having perceived the tumult; but Tommasino struck at them with the flat of his sword, and they gave way before the rushing horses; and before the great gate was shut, Antonio and he were on their way through, and the hoofs of their horses clattered over the bridge. Thus Antonio was clear of the city with his lady in his arms and Tommasino his cousin safe by his side.

Yet they were not safe; for neither Duke Valentine nor Robert de Beauregard was a man who sat down under defeat. But few moments had passed before there issued from the gate a company of ten mounted and armed men, and Robert, riding in their front, saw, hard on a mile away, the cousins heading across the plain towards the spot where the spurs of Mount Agnino run down; for there was the way of safety. But it was yet ten miles away. And Robert and his company galloped furiously in pursuit, while Duke Valentine watched from the wall of the garden above the river.

Now Count Antonio was a big man and heavy, so that his horse was weighed down by the twofold burden on its back; and looking behind him, he perceived that Robert's company drew nearer and yet nearer. And Tommasino, looking also, said, "I doubt they are too many for us, for you have the lady in your arms. We shall not get clear of the hills."

Then Antonio drew in his horse a little and, letting the bridle fall, took the Lady Lucia in both his arms and kissed her, and having thus done, lifted her and set her on Tommasino's horse. "Thank God," said he, "that you are no heavier than a feather."

"Yet two feathers may be too much," said Tommasino.

"Ride on," said Antonio. "I will check them for a time, so that you shall come safe to the outset of the hill."

Tommasino obeyed him; and Antonio, riding more softly now, placed himself between Tommasino and the pursuers. Tommasino rode on with the swooning lady in his arms; but his face was grave and troubled, for, as he said, two feathers may be overmuch, and Robert's company rode well and swiftly.

"If Antonio can stop them, it is well," said he; "but if not, I shall not reach the hills;"

and he looked with no great love on the unhappy lady, for it seemed like enough that Antonio would be slain for her sake, and Tommasino prized him above a thousand damsels. Yet he rode on, obedient.

But Antonio's scheme had not passed undetected by Robert de Beauregard; and Robert, being a man of guile and cunning, swore aloud an oath that, though he died himself, yet Tommasino should not carry off Lucia. Therefore he charged his men one and all to ride after Tommasino and bring back Lucia, leaving him alone to contend with Antonio; and they were not loth to obey, for it was little to their taste or wish to surround Antonio and kill him. Thus, when the company came within fifty yards of Antonio, the ranks suddenly parted; five diverged to the right, and four to the left, passing Antonio in sweeping curves, so far off that he could not reach them, while Robert alone rode straight at him. Antonio, perceiving the stratagem, would fain have ridden again after Tommasino; but Robert was hard upon him, and he was in peril of being thrust through the back as he fled. So he turned and faced his enemy. But although Robert had sworn so boldly before his men, his mind was not what he had declared to them, and he desired to meet Antonio alone, not that he might fight a fair fight with him, but in order treacherously to deceive him—a thing he was ashamed to do before his comrades. Coming up then to Antonio, he reined in his horse, crying, "My lord, I bring peace from His Highness."

Antonio wondered to hear him; yet, when Robert, his sword lying untouched in its sheath, sprang from his horse and approached him, he dismounted also; and Robert said to him: "I have charged them to injure neither the Lady Lucia nor your cousin by so much as a hair; for the Duke bids me say that he will not constrain the lady."

"Is she then given to me?" cried Antonio, his face lighting up with a marvellous eagerness.

"Nay, not so fast," answered Robert with subtle cunning. "The Duke will not give her to you now. But he will exact from you and from me alike an oath not to molest, no, not to see her, for three months, and then she shall choose as she will between us."

While he spoke this fair speech, he had been drawing nearer to Antonio; and Antonio, not yet convinced of his honesty, drew back a pace. Then Robert let go hold of his horse, unbuckled his sword, flung it on the ground, and came to Antonio with outstretched hands. "Behold!" said he; "I am in your mercy, my lord. If you do not believe me, slay me."

Antonio looked at him with searching wistful eyes; he hated to war against the Duke, and his heart was aflame with the hope that dwelt for him in Robert's words; for he did not doubt but that neither three months, nor three years, nor three hundred years, could change his lady's love.

"You speak fair, sir," said he; "but what warrant have I?"

"And, save your honour, what warrant have I, who stand here unarmed before you?" asked Robert.

For a while Antonio pondered; then he said,

"My lord, I must crave your pardon for my doubt; but the matter is so great that to your word I dare not trust; but if you will ride back with your men and pray the Duke to send me a promise under his own hand, to that I will trust. And meanwhile Tommasino, with the Lady Lucia, shall abide in a safe place, and I will stay here, awaiting your return; and, if you will, let two of your men stay with me."

"Many a man, my lord," returned Robert, "would take your caution in bad part. But let it be so. Come, we will ride after my company." And he rose and caught Antonio's horse by the bridle and brought it to him; "Mount, my lord," said he, standing by.

Antonio, believing either that the man was true or that his treachery—if treachery there were in him—was foiled, and seeing him to all seeming unarmed, save for a little dagger in his belt which would hardly suffice to kill a man and was more a thing of ornament than use, set his foot in the stirrup and prepared to mount. And in so doing he turned his back on Robert de Beauregard. The moment for which that wicked man had schemed and lied was come. Still holding Antonio's stirrup with one hand, he drew, swift as lightning, from under his cloak, a dagger different far from the toy in his belt— short, strong, broad, and keen. And that moment had been Antonio's last, had it not chanced that, on the instant Robert drew the dagger, the horse started a pace aside, and Antonio, taken unawares, stumbled forward and came near falling on the ground. His salvation lay in that stumble, for Robert, having put all his strength into the blow, and then striking not Antonio but empty air, in his turn staggered forward, and could not recover himself before Antonio turned round, a smile at his own unwariness on his lips.

Then he saw the broad keen knife in the hand of Robert. Robert breathed quickly, and glared at him, but did not rush on him. He stood glaring, the knife in his hands, his parted lips displaying grinning teeth. Not a word spoke Antonio, but he drew his sword, and pointed where Robert's sword lay on the grass. The traitor, recognising the grace that allowed him to take his sword, shamed, it may be, by such return for his own treachery, in silence lifted and drew it; and, withdrawing to a distance from the horses, which quietly cropped the grass, the two faced one another.

Calm and easy were the bearing and the air of Count Antonio, if the pictures of him that live drawn in the words of those who knew him be truthful; calm and easy ever was he, save when he fought; but then it seemed as though there came upon him a sort of fury akin to madness, or (as the ancients would have fabled) to some inspiration from the God of War, which transformed him utterly, imbuing him with a rage and rushing impetuosity. Here lay his danger when matched with such a swordsman as was little Tommasino; but for all that, few cared to meet him, some saying that, though they called themselves as brave as others, yet they seemed half appalled when Count Antonio set upon them; for he fought as though he must surely win and as though God were with him. Thus now he darted upon Robert de Beauregard, in seeming recklessness of receiving thrusts himself, yet ever escaping them by his sudden resource and dexterity and ever himself attacking, leaving no space to take breath, and bewildering the other's practised skill by the dash and brilliance of his assault. And it may be also that the darkness, which was now falling fast, hindered Robert the more, for Antonio was famed for the keenness of his eyes by night. Be these things as they may, in the very moment when Robert pricked Antonio in the left arm and cried out in triumph on his stroke, Antonio leapt on him and drove his sword through his heart; and Robert, with the sword yet in him, fell to the ground, groaning. And when Antonio drew forth the sword, the man at his feet died. Thus, if it be God's will, may all traitors perish.

Antonio looked round the plain; but it grew darker still, and even his sight did not avail for more than some threescore yards. Yet he saw a dark mass on his right, distant, as he judged, that space or more. Rapidly it moved: surely it was a group of men galloping, and Antonio stood motionless regarding them. But they swept on, not turning whither he stood; and he, unable to tell what they did, whether they sought him or whither they went, watched them till they faded away in the darkness; and then, leaving Robert where he lay, he mounted his horse and made speed towards the hills, praying that there he should find his cousin and the Lady Lucia, escaped from the pursuit of the Duke's men. Yet had he known what those dimly discerned riders bore with them, he would have been greatly moved at all costs and at every hazard to follow after them and seek to overtake them before they came to the city.

On he rode towards the hills, quickly, yet not so hastily but that he scanned the ground as he went so well as the night allowed him. The moon was risen now and to see was easier. When he had covered a distance of some two miles, he perceived something lying across his path. Bending to look, he found it to be the corpse of a horse: he leapt down and bent over it. It was the horse Tommasino had ridden; it was hamstrung, and its throat had been cut. Antonio, seeing it, in sudden apprehension of calamity, cried aloud; and to his wonder his cry was answered by a voice which came from a clump of bushes fifty yards on the right. He ran hastily to the spot, thinking nothing of his own safety nor of anything else than what had befallen his friends; and under the shelter of the bushes two men of the Duke's Guard, their horses tethered near them, squatted on the ground, and, between, Tommasino lay full length on the ground. His face was white, his eyes closed, and a bloody bandage was about his head. One of the two by him had forced his lips open and was giving him to drink from a bottle. The other sprang up on sight of Antonio and laid a hand to his sword-hilt.

"Peace, peace!" said Antonio. "Is the lad dead?"

"He is not dead, my lord, but he is sore hurt."

"And what do you here with him? And how did you take him?"

"We came up with him here, and surrounded him; and while some of us held him in front, one cut the hamstrings of his horse from behind; and the horse fell, and with the horse the lady and the young lord. He was up in an instant; but as he rose, the lieutenant struck him on the head and dealt him the wound you see. Then he could fight no more; and the lieutenant took the lady, and with the rest rode back towards the city, leaving us charged with the duty of bringing the young lord in so soon as he was in a state to come with us."

"They took the lady?"

"Even so, my lord."

"And why did they not seek for me?"

The fellow—Martolo was his name—smiled grimly; and his comrade, looking up, answered: "Maybe they did not wish to find you, my lord. They had been eight to one, and could not have failed to take you in the end."

"Aye, in the end," said Martolo, laughing now. "Nor," added he, "had the lieutenant such great love for Robert de Beauregard that he would rejoice to deliver you to death for his sake, seeing that you are a Monte Velluto and he a rascally——"

"Peace! He is dead," said Count Antonio.

"You have killed him?" they cried with one voice.

"He attacked me in treachery, and I have killed him," answered Antonio.

For a while there was silence. Then Antonio asked, "The lady—did she go willingly?"

"She was frightened and dazed by her fall, my lord; she knew not what she did nor what they did to her. And the lieutenant took her in front of him, and, holding her with all gentleness, so rode towards the city."

"God keep her," said Antonio.

"Amen, poor lady!" said Martolo, doffing his cap.

Then Antonio whistled to his horse, which came to his side; with a gesture he bade the men stand aside, and they obeyed him; and he gathered Tommasino in his arms. "Hold my stirrup, that I may mount," said he; and still they obeyed. But when they saw him mounted, with Tommasino seated in front of him, Martolo cried, "But, my lord, we are charged to take him back and deliver him to the Duke."

"And if you do?" asked Antonio.

Martolo made a movement as of one tying a noose.

"And if you do not?" asked Antonio.

"Then we had best not show ourselves alive to the Duke."

Antonio looked down on them. "To whom bear you allegiance?" said he.

"To His Highness the Duke," they answered, uncovering as they spoke.

"And to whom besides?" asked Antonio.

"To none besides," they answered, wondering.

"Aye, but you do," said he. "To One who wills not that you should deliver to death a lad who has done but what his honour bade him."

"God's counsel God knows," said Martolo. "We are dead men if we return alone to the city. You had best slay us yourself, my lord, if we may not carry the young lord with us."

"You are honest lads, are you not?" he asked. "By your faces, you are men of the city."

"So are we, my lord; but we serve the Duke in his Guard for reward."

"I love the men of the city as they love me,"

said Antonio. "And a few pence a day should not buy a man's soul as well as his body."

The two men looked at one another in perplexity. The fear and deference in which they held Antonio forbade them to fall on him; yet they dared not let him take Tommasino. Then, as they stood doubting, he spoke low and softly to them: "When he that should give law and uphold right deals wrong, and makes white black and black white, it is for gentlemen and honest men to be a law unto themselves. Mount your horses, then, and follow me. And so long as I am safe, you shall be safe; and so long as I live, you shall live; and while I eat and drink, you shall have to drink and eat; and you shall be my servants. And when the time of God's will—whereof God forbid that I should doubt—is come, I will go back to her I love, and you shall go back to them that love you; and men shall say that you have proved yourselves true men and good."

Thus it was that two men of the Duke's Guard—Martolo and he whom they called Bena (for of his true name there is no record)—went together with Count Antonio and his cousin Tommasino to a secret fastness in the hills; and there in the course of many days Tommasino was healed of the wound which the Lieutenant of the Guard had given him, and rode his horse again, and held next place to Antonio himself in the band that gathered round them. For there came to them every man that was wrongfully oppressed; and some came for love of adventure and because they hoped to strike good blows; and some came whom Antonio would not receive, inasmuch as they were greater rogues than were those whose wrath they fled from.

Such is the tale of how Count Antonio was outlawed from the Duke's peace and took to the hills. Faithfully have I set it down, and whoso will may blame the Count, and whoso will may praise him. For myself, I thank Heaven that I am well rid of this same troublesome passion of love that likens one man to a lion and another to a fox.

But the Lady Lucia, being brought back to the city by the Lieutenant of the Guard, was lodged in her own house, and the charge of her was commended by the Duke into the hands of a discreet lady; and for a while His Highness, for very shame, forbore to trouble her with suitors. For he said, in his bitter humour, as he looked down on the dead body of Robert de Beauregard: "I have lost two good servants and four strong arms through her; and mayhap, if I find her another suitor, she will rob me of yet another stalwart gentleman."

So she abode, in peace indeed, but in sore desolation and sorrow, longing for the day when Count Antonio should come back to seek her. And again was she closely guarded by the Duke.

CHAPTER II.

COUNT ANTONIO AND THE TRAITOR PRINCE.

OF all the deeds that Count Antonio of Monte Velluto did during the time that he was an outlaw in the hills (for a price had been set on his head by Duke Valentine), there was none that made greater stir or struck more home to the hearts of men, howsoever they chose to look upon it, than that which he performed on the high hill that faces the wicket gate on the west side of the city and is called now the Hill of Duke Paul. Indeed it was the act of a man whose own conscience was his sole guide, and who made the law which his own hand was to carry out. That it had been a crime in most men, who can doubt? That it was a crime in him, all governments must hold; and the same, I take it, must be the teaching of the Church.

Yet not all men held it a crime, although they had not ventured it themselves, both from the greatness of the person whom the deed concerned, and also for the burden that it put on the conscience of him that did it. Here, then, is the story of it, as it is still told both in the houses of the noble and in peasants' cottages.

While Count Antonio still dwelt at the Court, and had not yet fled from the wrath aroused in the Duke by the Count's attempt to carry off the Lady Lucia, the Duke's ward, the nuptials of His Highness had been celebrated with great magnificence and universal rejoicing; and the feasting and exultation had been most happily renewed on the birth of an infant Prince, a year later. Yet heavy was the price paid for this gift of Heaven, for Her Highness the Duchess, a lady of rare grace and kindliness, survived the birth of her son only three months, and then died, amidst the passionate mourning of the people, leaving the Duke a prey to bitter sorrow. Many say that she had turned his heart to good had she but lived, and that it was the loss of her that soured him

and twisted his nature. If it be so, I pray that
he has received pardon for all his sins; for his
grief was great, and hardly to be assuaged even
by the love he had for the little Prince, from
whom he would never be parted for an hour,
if he could contrive to have the boy with him,
and in whom he saw, with pride, the heir of his
throne.

Both in the joy of the wedding and the grief
at the Duchess's death, none had made more
ostentatious sign of sharing than His Highness's
brother, Duke Paul. Yet hollow alike were his
joy and his grief, save that he found true cause
for sorrow in that the Duchess left to her
husband a dear memorial of their brief union.
Paul rivalled the Duke in his caresses and his
affected love for the boy, but he had lived long
in the hope that His Highness would not marry,
and that he himself should succeed him in his
place, and this hope he could not put out of his
heart. Nay, as time passed and the baby grew
to a healthy boy, Paul's thoughts took a still
deeper hue of guilt. It was no longer enough
for him to hope for his nephew's death, or even

to meditate how he should bring it about. One wicked imagining led on, as it is wont in our sinful nature, to another, and Satan whispered in Paul's ear that the Duke himself was short of forty by a year, that to wait for power till youth were gone was not a bold man's part, and that to contrive the child's death, leaving his father alive, was but to double the risk without halving the guilt. Thus was Paul induced to dwell on the death of both father and son, and to say to himself that if the father went first the son would easily follow, and that with one cunning and courageous stroke the path to the throne might be cleared.

While Paul pondered on these designs, there came about the events which drove Count Antonio from the Court; and no sooner was he gone and declared in open disobedience and contumacy against the Duke, than Paul, seeking a handle for his plans, seemed to find one in Antonio. Here was a man driven from his house (which the Duke had burnt), despoiled of his revenues, bereft of his love, proclaimed a free mark for whosoever would serve the Duke by slaying him. Where could be a better man for the purposes of a malcontent prince? And the more was Paul inclined to use Antonio from the fact that he had shown favour to Antonio, and been wont to seek his society; so that Antonio, failing to pierce the dark depths of his heart, was loyally devoted to him, and had returned an answer full of gratitude and friendship to the secret messages in which Paul had sent him condolence on the mishap that had befallen him.

Now in the beginning of the second year of Count Antonio's outlawry, His Highness was most mightily incensed against him, not merely because he had so won the affection of the country-folk that none would betray his hiding-place either for threats or for reward, but most chiefly by reason of a certain act which was in truth more of Tommasino's doing than of Antonio's. For Tommasino, meeting one of the Duke's farmers of taxes, had lightened him of his fat bag of money, saying that he would himself assume the honour of delivering what was fairly due to His Highness, and had upon that scattered three-fourths of the spoil among the poor, and sent the beggarly remnant privily by night to the gate of the city, with a writing, "There is honour among thieves; who, then, may call Princes thieves?" And this writing had been read by many, and the report of it, spreading through the city, had made men laugh. Therefore the Duke had sworn that by no means should Antonio gain pardon save by delivering that insolent young robber to the hands of justice. Thus he was highly pleased when his brother sought him in the garden (for he sat in his wonted place under the wall by the fish-pond) and bade him listen to a plan whereby the outlaws should be brought to punishment. The Duke took his little son upon his knees and prayed his brother to tell his device.

"You could not bring me a sweeter gift than the head of Tommasino," said he, stroking the child's curls; and the child shrank closer into his arms, for the child did not love Paul but feared him.

"Antonio knows that I love Your Highness,"

said Paul, seating himself on the seat by the Duke, "but he knows also that I am his friend, and a friend to the Lady Lucia, and a man of tender heart. Would it seem to him deep treachery if I should go privately to him and tell him how that on a certain day you would go forth with your guard to camp in the spurs of Mount Agnino, leaving the city desolate, and that on the night of that day I could contrive that Lucia should come secretly to the gate, and that it should be opened for her, so that by a sudden descent she might be seized and carried safe to his hiding-place before aid could come from Your Highness?"

"But what should the truth be?" asked Valentine.

"The truth should be that while part of the Guard went to the spurs of the Mount, the rest should lie in ambush close inside the city gates and dash out on Antonio and his company."

"It is well, if he will believe."

Then Paul laid his finger on his brother's arm. "As the clock in the tower of the cathedral strikes three on the morning of the 15th of the month, do you, dear brother, be in your summer-house at the corner of the garden yonder; and I will come thither and tell you if he has believed and if he has come. For by then I shall have learnt from him his mind: and we two will straightway go rouse the guards and lead the men to their appointed station, and when he approaches the gate we can lay hands on him."

"How can you come to him? For we do not know where he is hid."

"Alas, there is not a rogue of a peasant that cannot take a letter to him!"

"Yet when I question them, aye, though I beat them, they know nothing!" cried Valentine in chagrin. "Truly, the sooner we lay him by the heels, the better for our security."

"Shall it be, then, as I say, my lord?"

"So let it be," said the Duke. "I will await you in the summer-house."

Paul, perceiving that his brother had no suspicions of him, and would await him in the summer-house, held his task to be already half done. For his plan was that he and Antonio should come together to the summer-house, but that Antonio should lie hid till Paul had spoken to the Duke; then Paul should go out on pretext of bidding the guard make ready the ambush, and leave the Duke alone with Antonio. Antonio then, suddenly springing forth, should slay the Duke; while Paul—and when he thought on this, he smiled to himself—would so contrive that a body of men should bar Antonio's escape, and straightway kill him. Thus should he be quit both of his brother and of Antonio, and no man would live who knew how the deed was contrived. "And then," said he, "I doubt whether the poor child, bereft of all parental care, will long escape the manifold perils of infancy."

Thus he schemed; and when he had made all sure, and noised about the Duke's intentions touching his going to the spurs of Mount Agnino, he himself set forth alone on his horse to seek Antonio. He rode till he reached the entrance of the pass leading to the recesses of the hills. There he dismounted, and sat down on the ground; and this was at noon on the 13th day of the month. He had not long been sitting, when a face peered from behind a wall of moss-covered rock that fronted him, and Paul cried, "Is it a friend?"

"A friend of whom mean you, my lord?" came from the rock.

"Of whom else than of Count Antonio?" cried Paul.

A silence followed and a delay; then two men stole cautiously from behind the rock, and in one of them Paul knew the man they called Bena, who had been of the Duke's Guard. The men, knowing Paul, bowed low to him, and asked him his pleasure, and he commanded them to bring him to Antonio. They wondered, knowing not whether he came from the Duke or despite the Duke; but he was urgent in his commands, and at length they tied a scarf over his eyes, and set him on his horse, and led the horse. Thus they went for an hour. Then they prayed him to dismount, saying that the horse could go no farther; and though Paul's eyes saw nothing, he heard the whinnying and smelt the smell of horses.

"Here are your stables then," said he, and dismounted with a laugh.

Then Bena took him by the hand, and the other guided his feet, and climbing up steep paths, over boulders and through little watercourses, they went, till at length Bena cried, "We are at home, my lord;" and Paul, tearing off his bandage, found himself on a small level spot, ringed round with stunted wind-beaten firs; and three huts stood in the middle of the space, and before one of the huts sat Tommasino, composing a sonnet to a pretty peasant girl whom he had chanced to meet that day; for Tommasino had ever a hospitable heart. But seeing Paul, Tommasino left his sonnet, and with a cry of wonder sprang to meet him; and Paul took him by both hands and saluted him. That night and the morning that followed, Paul abode with Antonio, eating the good cheer and drinking the good wine that Tommasino, who had charged himself with the care of such matters, put before him. Whence they came from, Paul asked not; nor did Tommasino say more than that they were offerings to Count Antonio—but whether offerings of free-will or necessity, he said not. And during this time Paul spoke much with Antonio privily and apart, persuading him of his friendship, and telling most pitiful things of the harshness shown by Valentine his brother to the Lady Lucia, and how the lady grew pale, and peaked and pined, so that the physicians knit their brows over her and the women said no drugs would patch a broken heart. Thus he inflamed Antonio's mind with a great rage against the Duke, so that he fell to counting the men he had and wondering whether there were force to go openly against the city. But in sorrow Paul answered that the pikemen were too many.

"But there is a way, and a better," said Paul, leaning his head near to Antonio's ear. "A way whereby you may come to your own again, and rebuild your house that the Duke has burnt, and enjoy the love of Lucia, and hold foremost place in the Duchy."

"What way is that?" asked Antonio in wondering eagerness. "Indeed I am willing to serve His Highness in any honourable service, if by that I may win his pardon and come to that I long for."

"His pardon! When did he pardon?" sneered Paul.

To know honest men and leave them to their honesty is the last great gift of villainy. But Paul had it not; and now he unfolded to Antonio the plan that he had made, saving (as needs not to be said) that part of it whereby Antonio himself was to meet his death. For a pretext he alleged that the Duke oppressed the city, and that he, Paul, was put out of favour because he had sought to protect the people, and was fallen into great suspicion. Yet, judging Antonio's heart by his own, he dwelt again and longer on the charms of Lucia, and on the great things he would give Antonio when he ruled the Duchy for his nephew; for of the last crime he meditated, the death of the child, he said naught then, professing to love the child. When the tale began, a sudden start ran through Antonio, and his face flushed; but he sat still and listened with unmoved face, his eyes gravely regarding Paul the while. No anger did he show, nor wonder, nor scorn, nor now any eagerness; but he gazed at the Prince with calm musing glance, as though he considered of some great question put before him. And when Paul ended his tale, Antonio sat yet silent and musing. But Paul was trembling now, and he stretched out his hand and laid it on Antonio's knee, and asked, with a feigned laugh that choked in the utterance, "Well, friend Antonio, is it a clever plan, and will you ride with me?"

Minute followed minute before Antonio answered. At length the frown vanished from his brow, and his face grew calm and set, and he answered Duke Paul, saying, "It is such a plan as you, my lord, alone of all men in the Duchy could make; and I will ride with you."

Then Paul, in triumph, caught him by the hands and pressed his hands, calling him a man of fine spirit and a true friend, who should not lack reward. And all this Antonio suffered silently; and in silence still he listened while Paul told him how that a path led privately from the bank of the river, through a secret gate in the wall, to the summer-house where the Duke was to be; of this gate he alone, saving the Duke had the key; they had but to swim the river and enter by this gate. Having hidden Antonio, Paul would talk with the Duke; then he would go and carry off what remained of the guard over and above those that were gone to the hills; and Antonio, having done his deed, could return by the same secret path, cross the river again, and rejoin his friends. And in a short space of time Paul would recall him with honour to the city and give him Lucia to wife.

"And if there be a question as to the hand that dealt the blow, there is a rascal whom the Duke flogged but a few days since, a steward in the palace. He deserves hanging, Antonio, for a thousand things of which he is guilty, and it will trouble me little to hang him for one whereof he chances to be innocent." And Duke Paul laughed heartily.

"I will ride with you," said Antonio again.

Then, it being full mid-day, they sat down to dinner, Paul bandying many merry sayings with Tommasino, Antonio being calm but not uncheerful. And when the meal was done, Paul drank to the good fortune of their expedition; and Antonio having drained his glass, said, "May God approve the issue," and straightway bade Tommasino and Martolo prepare to ride with him. Then, Paul being again blindfolded, they climbed down the mountain paths till they came where the horses were, and thus, as the sun began to decline, set forward, at a fair pace, Duke Paul and Antonio leading by some few yards; while Tommasino and Martolo, having drunk well, and sniffing sport in front of them, sang, jested, and played pranks on one another as they passed along. But when night fell they became silent; even Tommasino turned grave and checked his horse, and the space between them and the pair who led grew greater, so that it seemed to Duke Paul that he and Antonio rode alone through the night, under the shadows of the great hills. Once and again he spoke to Antonio, first of the scheme, then on some light matter; but Antonio did no more than move his head in assent. And Antonio's face was very white, and his lips were close shut.

It was midnight when Duke Paul and Antonio reached the plain: the moon, till now hidden by the mountains, shone on them, and, seeing Antonio's face more plainly, Paul cried, half in jest, half in uneasiness, 'Come, man, look not so glum about it! 'Tis but the life of a rogue."

"Indeed it is no more," said Antonio, and he turned his eyes on Duke Paul.

Paul laughed, but with poor merriment. Whence it came he knew not, but a strange sudden sense of peril and of doom had fallen on him. The massive quiet figure of Antonio, riding ever close to him, silent, stern, and watchful, oppressed his spirit.

Suddenly Antonio halted and called to Martolo to bring him a lantern: one hung from Martolo's saddle, and he brought it, and went back. Then Antonio lit the lantern and gave an ivory tablet to Paul and said to him, "Write me your promise."

"You distrust me, then?" cried Paul in a great show of indignation.

"I will not go till you have written the promise."

Now Paul was somewhat loth to write the promise, fearing that it should be found on Antonio's body before he could contrive to remove it; but without it Antonio declared he would not go. So Paul wrote, bethinking himself that he held safe in his house at home permission from the Duke to seek Antonio and beguile him to the city, and that with the witness of this commission he could come off safe, even though the tablet were found on Antonio. Taking the peril then, rather than fail, he wrote, setting out the promises he made to Antonio in case (thus he phrased it) of the death of his brother. And he delivered the tablet to Antonio; and Antonio, restoring the lantern to Martolo, stowed the tablet about him, and they set forth again.

As the clock in the tower of the cathedral, distantly booming in their ears, sounded the hour of two, they came to where the road parted. In one direction it ran level across the plain to the river and the city, and by this way they must go, if they would come to the secret gate and thence to the Duke's summer-house. But the second road left the plain, and mounted the hill that faces the wicket-gate, which is now called the Hill of Duke Paul. And at the parting of the road, Antonio reined in his horse and sat silent for a great while. Again Paul, scanning his face, was troubled, so that Martolo, who had drawn near, saw him wipe a drop from his brow. And Paul said, "For what wait we, Antonio? Time presses, for it has gone two o'clock."

Then Antonio drew him apart, and fixing his eyes on him, said, "What of the child? What mean you by the child? How does it profit you that the father die, if the child live?"

Paul, deeming that Antonio doubted him and saw a snare, and holding it better to seem the greatest of villains than to stir suspicion in a man who held him in his hands, smiled cunningly, and answered, "The child will grow sickly and pine when his father is not alive to care for him."

"It is enough," said Antonio; and again a flush mounted on his face, and died down again, and left him pale. For some think he would have turned from his purpose, had Paul meant honestly by the child. I know not. At least, the foul murder plotted against the child made him utterly relentless.

"Let us go on and end the matter," urged Paul, full of eagerness, and, again, of that strange uneasiness born of Antonio's air.

"Ay, we will go on and finish it," said Antonio, and with that he leapt down from his horse. Paul did the like, for it had been agreed that the others, with the horses, were to await Antonio's return, while the Count and Paul went forward on foot: and Tommasino and Martolo, dismounting also, tied the horses to trees and stood waiting Antonio's orders.

"Forward!" cried Paul.

"Come, then," said Antonio, and he turned to the road that mounted the hill.

"It is by the other road we go," said Paul.

"It is by this road," said Antonio, and he raised his hand and made a certain sign, whereat the swords of his friends leapt from their scabbards, and they barred the way, so that Duke Paul could turn nowhere save to the road that mounted the hill. Then Paul's face grew long, drawn, and sallow with sudden fear. "What means this?" he cried. "What means this, Antonio?"

"It means, my lord, that you must mount the hill with me," answered Antonio, "even to the top of it, whence a man can see the city."

"But for what?"

"That this matter may be finished," said Antonio; and, coming to Paul, he laid a hand on his shoulder and turned him to the path up the hill. But Paul, seeing his face and the swords of Tommasino and Martolo that barred all escape, seized his hand, saying, "Before God, I mean you true, Antonio! As Christ died for us, I mean you true, Antonio!"

"Of that I know not, and care not; yet do not swear it now by Christ's name if it be not true. How meant you, my lord, by your brother and your brother's son?"

Paul licked his lips, for they had gone dry, and he breathed as a man pants who has run far and fast. "You are three to one," he hissed.

"We shall be but man to man on the top of the hill," said Antonio.

Then suddenly Tommasino spoke unbidden. "There is a priest in the village a mile away," said he, and there was pity in his voice.

"Peace, Tommasino! What priest has he provided for his brother?"

And Tommasino said no more, but he turned his eyes away from the face of Duke Paul: yet when he was an old man, one being in his company heard him say he dreamed yet of it. As for Martolo, he bent his head and crossed himself.

Then Paul threw himself on his knees before Antonio and prayed him to let him go; but Antonio seemed not to hear him, and stood silent with folded arms. Yet presently he said, "Take your sword then, my lord. If I fall, these shall not touch you. This much I give, though it is more than I have right to give."

But Paul would not take his sword, but knelt, still beseeching Antonio with tears, and mingling prayers and curses in a flow of agonised words.

At last Antonio plucked him from the ground and sternly bade him mount the hill; and finding no help, he set out, his knees shaking beneath him, while Antonio followed close upon him. And thus Tommasino and Martolo watched them go till the winding of the path hid them from view, when Martolo fell on his knees, and Tommasino drew a breath as though a load had rested on his chest.

It was but a short way to the summit, but the path was steep, and the two went slowly, so that, as they came forth on the top, the first gleam of dawn caught them in its pale light. The city lay grey and drab below them, and the lonely tree, that stands to this day upon the hill, swayed in the wind with mournful murmurings. Paul stumbled and sank in a heap on the ground. And Antonio said to him, "If you will, pray," and went and leant against the bare trunk of the tree, a little way apart. But Paul, thinking on man's mercy, not on God's, crawled on his knees across the space between and laid hold of Antonio's legs. And he said nothing, but gazed up at Antonio. And at the silent appeal Antonio shivered for an instant, but he did not fly the gaze of Paul's eyes, but looked down on him and answered, "You must die. Yet there is your sword, and there a free road to the city."

Then Paul let go Antonio's legs and rose, and drew his sword. But his hand was trembling, and he could scarce stand. Then Antonio gave to him a flask that he carried, holding strong waters; and the wretch, drinking greedily, found some courage, and came suddenly at Antonio before Antonio looked for his attack. But the Count eluded him, and drawing his blade awaited the attack; and Paul seized again the flask that he had flung on the ground, and drained it, and mad now with the fumes rushed at Antonio, shrieking curses and blasphemies. The sun rose on the moment that their blades crossed; and before its rays had shone a minute, Antonio had driven his sword through the howling wretch's lung, and Duke Paul lay dying on the grassy hill.

Then Count Antonio stripped off his doublet and made a pillow of it for Paul's head, and sat down by him, and wiped his brow, and disposed his body with such ease as seemed possible. Yet he took no pains to stanch the blood or to minister to the wound, for his intent was that Paul should die and not live. And Paul lay some moments on his back, then twisted on his side; once he flung his legs wide and gathered them again under his body, and shivered, turning on his back again: and his jaw fell, and he died there on the top of the hill. And the Count closed his eyes, and sat by him in silence for many minutes; and once he buried his face in his hands, and a single sob shook him.

But now it was growing to day, and he rose, and took from the Duke's waist the broad silken band that he wore, wrought with golden embroidery on a ground of royal blue. Then he took Paul in his arms and set him upright against the trunk of the tree, and, encircling tree and body with the rich scarf, he bound the corpse there; and he took the ivory tablet from his belt and tied the riband that hung through a hole in it to the riband of the Order of St. Prisian, that was round Paul's neck, and he wrote on the tablet, "Witness my hand—ANTONIO of Monte Velluto." And he wiped the blade of his sword long and carefully on the grass till it shone pure, clean, and bright again. Then he gazed awhile at the city, that grew now warm and rich in the increasing light of the sun, and turned on his heel and went down the hill by the way that he had come.

At the foot, Tommasino and Martolo awaited him; and when he came down alone, Martolo again signed the cross; but Tommasino glanced one question, and, finding answer in Antonio's nod, struck his open palm on the quarters of Duke Paul's horse and set it free to go where it would; and the horse, being free, started at a canter along the road to the city. And Antonio mounted and set his face again towards the hills. For awhile he rode alone in front; but when an hour was gone, he called to Tommasino, and, on the lad joining him, talked with him, not gaily indeed (that could not be), yet with calmness and cheerfulness on the matters that concerned the band. But Paul's name did not cross his lips; and the manner in which he had dealt with Paul on the hill rested unknown till a later time, when Count Antonio formally declared it, and wrote with his own hand how Duke Paul had died. Thus, then, Count Antonio rode back to the hills, having executed on the body of Paul that which seemed to him right and just.

Long had Duke Valentine waited for his

brother in the summer-house and greatly wondered that he came not. And as the morning grew and yet Paul came not, the Duke feared that in some manner Antonio had detected the snare, and that he held Paul a prisoner; for it did not enter the Duke's mind that Antonio would dare to kill his brother. And when it was five o'clock, the Duke, heavy-eyed for want of sleep, left the summer-house, and having traversed the garden, entered his cabinet and flung himself on a couch there; and notwithstanding his uneasiness for his brother, being now very drowsy, he fell asleep. But before he had slept long, he was roused by two of his pages, who ran in crying that Duke Paul's horse had come riderless to the gate of the city. And the Duke sprang up, smiting his thigh, and crying, "If harm has come to him, I will not rest till I have Antonio's head." So he mustered a party of his guards, some on horseback and some on foot, and passed with all speed out of the city, seeking his brother, and vowing vengeance on the insolence of Count Antonio.

But the Duke was not first out of the city;

for he found a stream of townsmen flocking across the bridge; and at the end of the bridge was a gathering of men, huddled close round a peasant who stood in the centre. The pikemen made a way for His Highness; and when the peasant saw him, he ran to him, and resting his hand on the neck of the Duke's horse, as though he could scarce stand alone, he cried, pointing with his hand to the hill that rose to the west, "The Duke Paul, the Duke Paul!" And no more could he say.

"Give him a horse, one of you, and let another lead it," cried the Duke. "And forward, gentlemen, whither he points!"

Thus they set forth, and as they went, the concourse grew, some overtaking them from the city, some who were going on their business or for pleasure into the city turning and following after the Duke and his company. So that a multitude went after Valentine and the peasant, and they rode together at the head. And the Duke said thrice to the peasant, "What of my brother?" But the peasant, who was an old man, did but point again to the hill.

At the foot of the hill, all that had horses left them in charge of the boys who were of the party, for the Duke, presaging some fearful thing, would suffer none but grown men to mount with him; and thus they went forward afoot till they reached the grassy summit of the hill. And then the peasant sprang in front, crying, "There, there!" and all of them beheld the body of Duke Paul, bound to the tree by the embroidered scarf, his head fallen on his breast, and the ivory tablet hanging from the riband of the Order of St. Prisian. And a great silence fell on them all, and they stood gazing at the dead prince.

But presently Duke Valentine went forward alone; and he knelt on one knee and bowed his head, and kissed his brother's right hand. And a shout of indignation and wrath went up from all the crowd, and they cried, "Whose deed is this?" The Duke minded them not, but rose to his feet and laid his hand on the ivory tablet; and he perceived that it was written by Duke Paul; and he read what Paul had written to Antonio; how that he, the Duke, being dead,

Antonio should come to his own again, and wed Lucia, and hold foremost place in the Duchy. And, this read, the Duke read also the subscription of Count Antonio—" Witness my hand—ANTONIO of Monte Velluto." Then he was very amazed, for he had trusted his brother. Yet he did not refuse the testimony of the ivory tablet nor suspect any guile or deceit in Antonio. And he stood dry-eyed, looking on the dead face of Duke Paul. Then, turning round, he cried in a loud voice, so that every man on the hill heard him, "Behold the body of a traitor!" And men looked on him, and from him to the faces of one another, asking what he meant. But he spoke no other word, and went straightway down the hill, and mounted his horse again, and rode back to the city; and, having come to his palace, he sent for his little son, and went with him into the cabinet behind the great hall, where the two stayed alone together for many hours. And when the child came forth, he asked none concerning his uncle the Duke Paul.

Now all the company had followed down

from the hill after the Duke, and no man dared to touch the body unbidden. Two days passed, and a great storm came, so that the rain beat on Paul's face and the lightning blackened it. But on the third day, when the storm had ceased, the Duke bade the Lieutenant of the Guard to go by night and bring the body of Paul: and the Lieutenant and his men flung a cloak over the face, and, having thus done, brought the body into the city at the break of day: yet the great square was full of folk watching in awe and silence. And they took the body to the Cathedral, and buried it under the wall on the north side in the shade of a cypress tree, laying a plain flat stone over it. And Duke Valentine gave great sums for masses to be said for the repose of his brother's soul. Yet there are few men who will go by night to the Hill of Duke Paul; and even now when I write, there is a man in the city who has lost his senses and is an idiot: he, they say, went to the hill on the night of the 15th of the month wherein Paul died, and came back mumbling things terrible to hear. But whether he went because he lacked his senses, or lost his senses by reason of the thing he saw when he went, I know not.

Thus died Duke Paul the traitor. Yet, though the Duke his brother knew that what was done upon him was nothing else than he had deserved and should have suffered had he been brought alive to justice, he was very wroth with Count Antonio, holding it insolence that any man should lay hands on one of his blood, and, of his own will, execute sentence upon a criminal of a degree so exalted. Therefore he sent word to Antonio, that if he caught him, he would hang him on the hill from the branches of the tree to which Antonio had bound Paul, and would leave his body there for three times three days. And, this message coming to Antonio, he sent one privily by night to the gate of the city, who laid outside the gate a letter for the Duke; and in the letter was written, "God chooses the hand. All is well."

And Count Antonio abode still an outlaw in the mountains, and the Lady Lucia mourned in the city.

CHAPTER III.

COUNT ANTONIO AND THE PRINCE OF MANTIVOGLIA.

I KNOW of naught by which a man may better be judged than by his bearing in matters of love. What know I of love, say you—I, whose head is grey, and shaven to boot? True, it is grey, and it is shaven. But once it was brown, and the tonsure came not there till I had lived thirty years and borne arms for twelve. Then came death to one I loved, and the tonsure to me. Therefore, O ye proud young men and laughing girls, old Ambrose knows of love, though his knowledge be only like the memory that a man has of a glorious red-gold sunset which his eyes saw a year ago: cold are the tints, gone the richness, sober and faint the picture. Yet it is something; he sees no more, but he has seen; and sometimes still I seem to see a face that last I saw smiling in death. They tell me such thoughts are not fitting in me, but I doubt their doing a man much harm; for they make him take joy when others reap the happiness that he, forestalled by fate's sickle, could not garner. But enough! It is of Count Antonio I would write, and not of my poor self. And the story may be worth the reading—or would be, had I more skill to pen it.

Now in the summer of the second year of Count Antonio's banishment, when the fierce anger of Duke Valentine was yet hot for the presumption shown by the Count in the matter of Duke Paul's death, a messenger came privily to where the band lay hidden in the hills, bringing greeting to Antonio from the Prince of Mantivoglia, between whom and the Duke there was great enmity. For in days gone by Firmola had paid tribute to Mantivoglia, and this burden had been broken off only some thirty years; and the Prince, learning that Antonio was at variance with Duke Valentine, perceived an opportunity, and sent to Antonio, praying him very courteously to visit Mantivoglia and be his guest. Antonio, who knew the Prince well, sent him thanks, and, having made dispositions for the safety of his company and set Tommasino in charge of it, himself rode with the man they called Bena, and, having crossed the frontier, came on the second day to Mantivoglia. Here he was received with great state, and all in the city were eager to see him, having heard how he had dealt with Duke Paul and how he now renounced the authority of Valentine. And the Prince lodged him in his palace, and prepared a banquet for him, and set him on the right hand of the Princess, who was a very fair lady, learned, and of excellent wit; indeed, I have by me certain stories which she composed, and would read on summer evenings in the garden; and it may be that, if I live, I will make known certain of them. Others there are that only the discreet should read; for what to one age is but mirth turns in the mind of the next to unseemliness and ribaldry. This Princess, then, was very gracious to the Count, and spared no effort to give him pleasure; and she asked him very many things concerning the Lady Lucia, saying at last, "Is she fairer than I, my lord?" But Antonio answered, with a laugh, "The moon is not fairer than the sun, nor the sun than the moon: yet they are different." And the Princess laughed also, saying merrily, "Well parried, my lord!" And she rose and went with the Prince and Antonio into the garden. Then the Prince opened to Antonio what was in his mind, saying, "Take what command you will in my service, and come with me against Firmola; and when we have brought Valentine to his knees, I will take what was my father's, and should be mine: and you shall wring from him your pardon and the hand of your lady." And the Princess also entreated him. But Antonio answered, "I cannot do it. If Your Highness rides to Firmola, it is likely enough that I also may ride thither; but I shall ride to put my sword at the service of the Duke. For, although he is not my friend, yet his enemies are mine." And from this they could not turn him. Then the Prince praised him, saying, "I love you more for denying me, Antonio; and when I send word of my coming to

Valentine, I will tell him also of what you have done. And if we meet by the walls of Firmola, we will fight like men; and, after that, you shall come again to Mantivoglia;" and he drank wine with Antonio, and so bade him God-speed. And the Princess, when her husband was gone, looked at the Count and said, "Valentine will not give her to you. Why will not you take her?"

But Antonio answered: "The price is too high."

"I would not have a man who thought any price too high," cried the Princess.

"Then your Highness would mate with a rogue?" asked Count Antonio, smiling.

"If he were one for my sake only," said she, fixing her eyes on his face and sighing lightly, as ladies sigh when they would tell something, and yet not too much nor in words that can be repeated. But Antonio kissed her hand, and took leave of her; and with another sigh she watched him go.

But when the middle of the next month came, the Prince of Mantivoglia gathered an army of three thousand men, of whom seventeen hundred were mounted, and crossed the frontier, directing his march towards Firmola by way of the base of Mount Agnino and the road to the village of Rilano. The Duke, hearing of his approach, mustered his Guards to the number of eight hundred and fifty men, and armed besides hard upon two thousand of the townsmen and apprentices, taking an oath of them that they would serve him loyally; for he feared and distrusted them; and of the whole force, eleven hundred had horses. But Count Antonio lay still in the mountains, and did not offer to come to the Duke's aid.

"Will you not pray his leave to come and fight for him?" asked Tommasino.

"He will love to beat the Prince without my aid, if he can," said Antonio. "Heaven forbid that I should seem to snatch at glory, and make a chance for myself from his necessity."

So he abode two days where he was; and then there came a shepherd, who said, "My lord, the Duke has marched out of the city and lay last night at Rilano, and is to-day stretched across the road that leads from the spurs of Agnino to

Rilano, his right wing resting on the river. There he waits the approach of the Prince; and they say that at daybreak to-morrow the Prince will attack."

Then Antonio rose, saying, "What of the night?"

Now the night was very dark, and the fog hung like a grey cloak over the plain. And Antonio collected all his men to the number of threescore and five, all well-armed and well-horsed; and he bade them march very silently and with great caution, and led them down into the plain. And all the night they rode softly, husbanding their strength and sparing their horses; and an hour before the break of day they passed through the outskirts of Rilano and halted a mile beyond the village, seeing the fires of the Duke's bivouacs stretched across the road in front of them; and beyond there were other fires where the Prince of Mantivoglia lay encamped. And Bena said, "The Prince will be too strong for the Duke, my lord."

"If he be, we also shall fight to-morrow, Bena," answered Antonio.

"I trust, then, that they prove at least well matched," said Bena; for he loved to fight, and yet was ashamed to wish that the Duke should be defeated.

Then Count Antonio took counsel with Tommasino; and they led the band very secretly across the rear of the Duke's camp till they came to the river. There was a mill on the river, and by the mill a great covered barn where the sacks of grain stood; and Antonio, having roused the miller, told him that he came to aid the Duke, and not to fight against him, and posted his men in this great barn; so that they were behind the right wing of the Duke's army, and were hidden from sight. Day was dawning now: the camp-fires paled in the growing light, and the sounds of preparation were heard from the camp. And from the Prince's quarters also came the noise of trumpets calling the men to arms.

At four in the morning the battle was joined, Antonio standing with Tommasino and watching from the mill. Now Duke Valentine had placed his own guards on either wing, and the townsmen in the centre; but the Prince had posted the flower of his troops in the centre; and he rode there himself, surrounded by many lords and gentlemen; and with great valour and impetuosity he flung himself against the townsmen, recking little of how he fared on either wing. This careless haste did not pass unnoticed by the Duke, who was a cool man and wore a good head; and he said to Lorenzo, one of his lords who was with him, "If we win on right and left, it will not hurt us to lose in the middle;" and he would not strengthen the townsmen against the Prince, but rather drew off more of them, and chiefly the stoutest and best equipped, whom he divided between the right wing where he himself commanded, and the left which Lorenzo led. Nay, men declare that he was not ill-pleased to see the brunt of the strife and the heaviest loss fall on the apprentices and townsmen. For a while indeed these stood bravely; but the Prince's chivalry came at them in fierce pride and gallant scorn, and bore them down with the weight of armour and horses, the Prince himself leading on a white charger and with his own hand slaying Glinka, who was head of the city-bands and a great champion among them. But Duke Valentine and Lorenzo upheld the battle on the wings, and pressed back the enemy there; and the Duke would not send aid to the townsmen in the centre, saying "I shall be ready for the Prince as soon as the Prince is ready for me, and I can spare some of those turbulent apprentices." And he smiled his crafty smile, adding, "From enemies also a wise man may suck good;" and he pressed forward on the right fighting more fiercely than was his custom. But when Antonio beheld the townsmen hard pressed and being ridden down by the Prince of Mantivoglia's knights and saw that the Duke would not aid them, he grew very hot and angry, and said to Tommasino, "These men have loved my house, Tommasino. It may be that I spoil His Highness's plan, but are we to stand here while they perish?"

"A fig for His Highness's plan!" said Tommasino; and Bena gave a cry of joy and sprang, unbidden, on his horse.

"Since you are up, Bena," said the Count, "stay up, and let the others mount. The Duke's plan, if I read it aright, is craftier than I love, and I do not choose to understand it."

Then, when the townsmen's line was giving way before the Prince, and the apprentices, conceiving themselves to be shamefully deserted, were more of a mind to run away than to fight any more, suddenly Antonio rode forth from the mill. He and his company came at full gallop; but he himself was ten yards ahead of Bena and Tommasino, for all that they raced after him. And he cried aloud, "To me, men of Firmola, to me, Antonio of Monte Velluto!" and they beheld him with utter astonishment and great joy. For his helmet was fallen from his head, and his fair hair gleamed in the sun, and the light of battle played on his face. And the band followed him, and, though they had for the most part no armour, yet such was the fury of their rush, and such the mettle and strength of their horses, that they made light of meeting the Prince's knights in full tilt. And the townsmen cried, "It is the Count! To death after the Count!" And Antonio raised the great sword that he carried, and rode at the Marshal of the

Prince's palace, who was in the van of the fight, and he split helmet and head with a blow. Then he came to where the Prince himself was, and the great sword was raised again, and the Prince rode to meet him, saying, "If I do not die now, I shall not die to-day." But when Antonio saw the Prince, he brought his sword to his side and bowed and turned aside, and engaged the most skilful of the Mantivoglian knights. And he fought that day like a man mad; but he would not strike the Prince of Mantivoglia. And after a while the Prince ceased to seek him; and a flatterer said to the Prince, "He is bold against us, but he fears you, my lord." But the Prince said, "Peace, fool. Go and fight." For he knew that not fear, but friendship, forbade Antonio to assail him.

Yet by now the rout of the townsmen was stayed and they were holding their own again in good heart and courage, while both on the right and on the left the Duke pressed on and held the advantage. Then the Prince of Mantivoglia perceived that he was in a dangerous plight, for he was in peril of being worsted along his whole line; for his knights did no more than hold a doubtful balance against the townsmen and Antonio's company, while the Duke and Lorenzo were victorious on either wing; and he knew that if the Duke got in rear of him and lay between him and Mount Agnino, he would be sore put to it to find a means of retreat. Therefore he left the centre and rode to the left of his line and himself faced Duke Valentine. Yet slowly was he driven back, and he gave way sullenly, obstinately, and in good order, himself performing many gallant deeds, and seeking to come to a conflict with the Duke. But the Duke, seeing that the day was likely to be his, would not meet him and chose to expose his person to no more danger: "For," he said, "a soldier who is killed is a good soldier; but a chief who is killed save for some great object is a bad chief." And he bided his time and slowly pressed the Prince back, seeking rather to win the battle than the praise of bravery. But when Count Antonio saw that all went well, and that the enemy were in retreat, he halted his band; and at this they murmured, Bena daring to say, "My lord, we have had dinner, and may we not have supper also?" Antonio smiled at Bena, but would not listen.

"No," said he. "His Highness has won the victory by his skill and cunning. I did but move to save my friends. It is enough. Shall I seek to rob him of his glory? For the ignorant folk, counting the arm more honourable than the head, will give me more glory than him if I continue in the fight." And thus, not being willing to force his aid on a man who hated to receive it, he drew off his band. Awhile he waited; but when he saw that the Prince was surely beaten, and that the Duke held victory in his hand, he gave the word that they should return by the way they had come.

"Indeed," said Tommasino, laughing, "it may be wisdom as well as good manners, cousin. For I would not trust myself to Valentine if he be victorious, for all the service which we have done him in saving the apprentices he loves so well."

So Antonio's band turned and rode off from the field, and they passed through Rilano. But they found the village desolate; for report had come from the field that the Duke's line was broken, and that in a short space the Prince of Mantivoglia would advance in triumph, and having sacked Rilano, would go against Firmola, where there were but a few old men and boys left to guard the walls against him. And one peasant, whom they found hiding in the wood by the road, said there was panic in the city, and that many were escaping from it before the enemy should appear.

"It is months since I saw Firmola," said Antonio with a smile. "Let us ride there and reassure these timid folk. For my lord the Duke has surely by now won the victory, and he will pursue the Prince till he yields peace and abandons the tribute."

Now a great excitement rose in the band at these words; for although they had lost ten men in the battle and five more were disabled, yet they were fifty stout and ready; and it was not likely that there was any force in Firmola that could oppose them. And Martolo, who rode with Tommasino, whispered to him, "My lord, my lord, shall we carry off the Lady Lucia before His Highness can return?"

Tommasino glanced at Antonio. "Nay, I know not what my cousin purposes," said he.

Then Antonio bade Bena and Martolo ride on ahead, taking the best horses, and tell the people at Firmola that victory was with the Duke, and that His Highness's servant, Antonio of Monte Velluto, was at hand to protect the city till His Highness should return in triumph. And the two, going ahead while the rest of the band took their mid-day meal, met many ladies and certain rich merchants and old men escaping from the city, and turned them back, saying that all was well; and the ladies would fain have gone on and met Antonio; but the merchants, hearing that he was there, made haste to get within the walls again, fearing that he would levy a toll on them for the poor, as his custom was. At this Bena laughed mightily, and drew rein, saying, "These rabbits will run quicker back to their burrow than we could ride, Martolo. Let us rest awhile under a tree; I have a flask of wine in my saddle-bag." So they rested; and while they rested, they saw what amazed them; for a lady rode alone towards them on a palfrey, and though the merchants met her and spoke with her, yet she rode on. And when she came to the tree where Bena and Martolo were, they sprang up and bared their heads; for she was the Lady Lucia; and her face was full of fear and eagerness as she said, "No guard is kept to-day, even on helpless ladies. Is it true that my lord is near?"

"Yes, he is near," said Bena, kissing her hand. "See, there is the dust of his company on the road."

"Go, one of you, and say that I wait for him," she commanded; so Martolo rode on to carry the news farther, and Bena went to Antonio and said, "Heaven, my lord, sends fortune. The Lady Lucia has escaped from the city, and awaits you under yonder tree."

And when Tommasino heard this, he put out his hand suddenly and caught Antonio's hand and pressed it, saying, "Go alone, and bring her here: we will wait: the Duke will not be here for many hours yet."

Then Antonio rode alone to the tree where Lucia was; and because he had not seen her for many months, he leapt down from his horse and came running to her, and, kneeling, kissed her hand; but she, who stood now by her palfrey's side, flung her arms about his neck and fell with tears and laughter into his arms, saying, "Antonio, Antonio! Heaven is with us, Antonio."

"Yes," said he. "For His Highness has won the day."

"Have not we won the day also?" said she, reaching up and laying her hands on his shoulders.

"Heart of my heart," said he softly, as he looked in her eyes.

"The cage is opened, and, Antonio, the bird is free," she whispered, and her eyes danced and her cheek went red. "Lift me to my saddle, Antonio."

The Count obeyed her, and himself mounted; and she said, "We can reach the frontier in three hours, and there—there, Antonio, none fears the Duke's wrath." And Antonio knew what she would say, save that she would not speak it bluntly—that there they could find a priest to marry them. And his face was pale as he smiled at her. Then he laid his hand on her bridle and turned her palfrey's head towards Firmola. Her eyes darted a swift question at him, and she cried low, "Thither, Antonio?"

Then he answered her, bending still his look on her, "Alas, I am no learned man, nor a doctor skilled in matters of casuistry and nice distinctions. I can but do what the blood that is in me tells me a gentleman should do. To-day, sweetheart—ah, will you not hide your face from me, sweetheart, that my words may not die in my mouth?—to-day our lord the Duke fights against the enemies of our city, holding for us in hard battle the liberty that we have won, and bearing the banner of Firmola high to heaven in victory."

She listened with strained frightened face; and the horses moved at a walk towards Firmola. And she laid her hand on his arm, saying again, "Antonio!"

"And I have fought with my lord to-day, and I would be at his side now, except that I do his pleasure better by leaving him to triumph alone.

But my hand has been with him to-day, and my heart is with him to-day. Tell me, sweetheart, if I rode forth to war and left you alone, would you do aught against me till I returned?"

She did not answer him.

"A Prince's city," said he, "should be as his faithful wife; and when he goes to meet the enemy, none at home should raise a hand against him; above all may not one who has fought by his side. For to stand side by side in battle is a promise and a compact between man and man, even as though man swore to man on a holy relic."

Then she understood what he would say, and she looked away from him across the plain; and a tear rolled down her cheek as she said, "Indeed, my lord, the error lies in my thoughts; for I fancied that your love was mine."

Antonio leant from his saddle and lightly touched her hair. "Was that indeed your fancy?" said he. "And I prove it untrue?"

"You carry me back to my prison," she said. "And you will ride away."

"And so I love you not?" he asked.

"No, you love me not," said she; and her voice caught in a sob.

"See," said he; "we draw near to Firmola, and the city gates are open; and, look, they raise a flag on the Duke's palace; and there is joy for the victory that Martolo has told them of. And in all the Duchy there are but two black hearts that burn with treacherous thoughts against His Highness, setting their own infinite joy above the honour and faith they owe him."

"Nay, but are there two?" she asked, turning her face from him.

"In truth I would love to think there was but one," said he. "And that one beats in me, sweetheart, and so mightily, that I think it will burst the walls of my body, and I shall die."

"Yet we ride to Firmola," said she.

"Yet, by Christ's grace," said Count Antonio, "we ride to Firmola."

Then the Lady Lucia suddenly dropped her bridle on the neck of her palfrey and caught Antonio's right hand in her two hands and said to him, "When I pray to-night, I will pray for

the cleansing of the black heart, Antonio. And
I will make a wreath and carry it to the Duke
and kiss his hand for his victory. And I will
set lights in my window and flags on my house;
and I will give my people a feast; and I will
sing and laugh for the triumph of the city and
for the freedom this day has won for us: and
when I have done all this, what may I do then,
Antonio?"

"I am so cruel," said he, "that then I would
have you weep a little: yet spoil not the loveliest
eyes in all the world; for if you dim them, it
may be that they will not shine like stars across
the plain and even into the hut where I live
among the hills."

"Do they shine bright, Antonio?"

"As the gems on the Gates of Heaven," he
answered; and he reined in his horse and gave
her bridle into her hands. And then for many
minutes neither spoke; and Count Antonio
kissed her lips, and she his; and they promised
with the eyes what they needed not to promise
with the tongue. And the Lady Lucia went
alone on her way to Firmola. But the Count

sat still like a statue of marble on his horse, and watched her as she rode. And there he stayed till the gates of the city received her and the walls hid her from his sight; and the old men on the walls saw him and knew him, and asked, "Does he come against us? But it was against the Prince of Mantivoglia that we swore to fight." And they watched him till he turned and rode at a foot's pace away from the city. And now as he rode his brow was smooth and calm and there was a smile on his lips.

But when Antonio had ridden two or three miles and came where he had left the band, he could see none of them. And a peasant came running to him in great fright and said, "My lord, your men are gone again to aid the Duke; for the Prince has done great deeds, and turned the fight, and it is again very doubtful: and my lord Tommasino bade me say that he knew your mind, and was gone to fight for Firmola."

Then Antonio, wondering greatly at the news, set his horse to a gallop and passed through Rilano at furious speed, and rode on towards Agnino; and it was now afternoon. Presently he saw the armies, but they seemed to lie idle, over against one another. And, riding on, he met Bena, who was come to seek him. And Bena said, "The Prince and his knights have fought like devils, my lord, and the townsmen grew fearful again when you were gone; and we, coming back, have fought again. But now a truce has sounded, and the Prince and the Duke are meeting in conference between the armies. Yet they say that no peace will be made; for the Prince, taking heart from his sudden success, though he is willing to abandon the tribute, asks something in return which the Duke will not grant. Yet perhaps he has granted it by now, for his men are weary."

"He should grant nothing," cried Antonio, and galloped on again. But Bena said to himself with an oath, "He has sent back the lady! The saints save us!" and followed Antonio with a laugh on his face.

But Antonio, thinking nothing of his own safety, rode full into the ranks of the Duke's Guard, saying, "Where does my lord talk with the Prince?" And they showed him where the place was; for the Prince and the Duke sat alone under a tree between the two arrays. And the Duke looked harsh and resolute, while the Prince was very courteously entreating him.

"Indeed," said he, "so doubtful has the day been, my lord, that I might well refuse to abandon the tribute, and try again to-morrow the issue of the fight. But, since so many brave men have fallen on both sides, I am willing to abandon it, asking of you only such favour as would be conceded to a simple gentleman asking of his friend. And yet you will not grant it me, and thus bring peace between us and our peoples."

Duke Valentine frowned and bit his lip; and the Prince rose from where he had been seated, and lifted his hand to the sky, and said, "So be it, my lord; on your head lies the blame. For to-morrow I will attack again; and, as God lives, I will not rest till the neck of the city of Firmola is under my foot, or my head rolls from my shoulders by your sword."

Then Duke Valentine paced up and down, pondering deeply. For he was a man that hated to yield aught, and beyond all else hated what the Prince of Mantivoglia asked of him. Yet he feared greatly to refuse; for the townsmen had no stomach for another fight and had threatened to march home if he would not make peace with the Prince. Therefore he turned to the Prince, and, frowning heavily, was about to say, "Since it must be so, so let it be," when suddenly the Count Antonio rode up and leapt from his horse, crying, "Yield nothing, my lord, yield nothing! For if you will tell me what to do, and suffer me to be your hand, we will drive the enemy over our borders with great loss."

Then the Prince of Mantivoglia fell to laughing, and he came to Antonio and put his arm about his neck, saying, "Peace, peace, thou foolish man!"

Antonio saluted him with all deference, but he answered, "I must give good counsel to my lord the Duke." And he turned to the Duke again, saying, "Yield nothing to the Prince, my lord."

Duke Valentine's lips curved in his slow smile as he looked at Antonio. "Is that indeed your counsel? And will you swear, Antonio, to give me your aid against the Prince so long as the war lasts, if I follow it?"

"Truly, I swear it," cried Antonio. "Yet what need is there of an oath? Am I not Your Highness's servant, bound to obey without an oath?"

"Nay, but you do not tell him——" began the Prince angrily.

Duke Valentine smiled again; he was ever desirous to make a show of fairness where he risked nothing by it; and he gazed a moment on Antonio's face; then he answered to the Prince of Mantivoglia, "I know the man, my lord. I know him in his strength and in his folly. Do not we know one another, Antonio?"

"Indeed, I know not all your Highness's mind," answered Antonio.

"Well, I will tell him," said Duke Valentine. "This Prince, Antonio, has consented to a peace, and to abandon all claim to tribute from our city, on one condition; which is, that I, the Duke, shall do at his demand what of my own free and sovereign will I would not do."

"His demand is not fitting nor warranted by

his power," said Antonio; but in spite of his words the Prince of Mantivoglia passed his arm through his, and laughed ruefully, whispering, "Peace, man, peace."

"And thus I, the Duke, having bowed my will to his, shall return to Firmola, not beaten indeed, yet half-beaten and cowed by the power of Mantivoglia."

"It shall not be, my lord," cried Count Antonio.

"Yet, my lord Duke, you do not tell him what the condition is," said the Prince.

"Why, it is nothing else than that I should pardon you, and suffer you to wed the Lady Lucia," said Duke Valentine.

Then Count Antonio loosed himself from the arm of the Prince and bent and kissed the Prince's hand; but he said, "Is this thing to come twice on a man in one day? For it is but an hour or less that I parted from the lady of whom you speak; and if her eyes could not move me, what else shall move me?" And he told them briefly of his meeting with the Lady Lucia. But Duke Valentine was wroth with the shame that a generous act rouses in a heart that knows no generosity; and the Prince was yet more wroth, and he said to Duke Valentine, "Were there any honour in you, my lord, you would not need my prayers to pardon him."

At this the Duke's face grew very dark; and he cried angrily, "Get back to your own line, my lord, or the truce shall not save you." And he turned to Antonio and said, "Three hours do I give you to get hence, before I pursue."

Antonio bowed low to him and to the Prince; and they three parted, the two princes in bitter wrath, and set again on fighting to the end, the one because he was ashamed and yet obstinate, the other for scorn of a rancour that found no place in himself. But Count Antonio went back to his company and drew it some little way off from both armies; and he said to Tommasino, "The truce is ended, and they will fight again so soon as the men have had some rest;" and he told Tommasino what had passed. Then he sat silent again; but presently he laid hold of his cousin's arm, saying, "Look you, Tommasino, princes are sometimes fools; and hence come trouble and death to honest humble folk. It is a sore business that they fight again to-morrow, and not now for any great matter, but because they are bitter against one another on my account. Cannot I stop them, Tommasino?"

"Aye, if you have five thousand men and not thirty-five—for that is the sum of us now, counting Martolo, who is back from Firmola."

Antonio looked thoughtfully through the dusk of evening which now fell. "They will not fight to-night," he said. "I am weary of this blood-letting." And Tommasino saw that there was something in his mind.

Now the night fell dark again and foggy, even as the night before; and none in either army dared to move, and even the sentries could see no more than a few yards before them. But Antonio's men being accustomed to ride in the dark, and to find their way through mists both in plain and hill, could see more clearly; and Antonio divided them into two parties, himself leading one, and giving the other into Tommasino's charge. Having very securely tethered their horses, they set forth, crawling on their bellies through the grass. Antonio with his party made for the camp of the Prince, while Tommasino and his party directed their way towards the Duke's bivouacs. And they saw the fires very dimly through the mist, and both parties passed the sentries unobserved, and made their way to the centre of the camps. Then, on the stroke of midnight, a strange stir arose in both the camps. Nothing could be seen by reason of the darkness and the mist; but suddenly cries arose, and men ran to and fro; and a cry went up from the Duke's camp, "They are behind us! They are behind us! We are surrounded!" And in the Prince's camp also was great fear; for from behind them, towards where the spurs of Mount Agnino began, there came shouts of "At them, at them! Charge!" And the Prince's officers, perceiving the cries to be from men of Firmola (and this they knew by reason of certain differences in the phrasing of words), conceived that the Duke had got behind them, and was lying across their way of retreat.

Then the Duke, hearing the shouts in his own camp, ran out from his tent; and he was met by hundreds of the townsmen, who cried, "My lord, we are surrounded!" For Antonio's men had gone to the townsmen and shewn them how they might escape more fighting; and the townsmen were nothing loth; and they insisted with the Duke that a body of men on horseback had passed behind them. So the Duke sent out scouts, who could see nothing of the horsemen. But then the townsmen cried, some being in the secret, others not, "Then they have ridden past us, and are making for Firmola. And they will do Heaven knows what there. Lead us after them, my lord!" And the Duke was very angry; but he was also greatly afraid, for he perceived that there was a stir in the Prince's camp also, and heard shouts from there, but could not distinguish what was said. And while he considered what to do, the townsmen formed their ranks and sent him word that they were for Firmola; and when he threatened them with his Guard, they rejoined that one death was as good as another; and the Duke gnawed his nails and went pale with rage. But Count Antonio's men, seeing how well the plan had sped, crept again out from the camp, and returned to where they had tethered their horses, and mounted, each taking a spare horse. And before they had been there long, they heard trumpets sound in the Duke's camp, and the camp was struck, and the Duke and all his force began to retreat on Rilano, throwing out many scouts, and moving very cautiously in the darkness and mist. Yet when they came on nobody, they marched more quickly, even the Duke himself now believing that the Prince of Mantivoglia had of a purpose allowed the stir in his camp to be seen and heard, in order that he might detach a column to Firmola unobserved, and attack the city before the Duke came up. Therefore he now pressed on, saying, "I doubt not that the Prince himself is with the troop that has gone to Firmola." And all night long they marched across the plain, covering a space of eighteen miles; and just before the break of day they came to the city.

Thus did it fall out with the army of Duke Valentine. But the Prince of Mantivoglia had been no less bewildered; for when he sent out men to see what the cries behind the camp meant, he found no man; but he still heard scattered cries among the rising ground, where the hills began. And he in his turn saw a stir in the camp opposite to him. And, being an impetuous Prince, as he had shown both in evil and in good that day, he snatched up his sword, swearing that he would find the truth of the matter, and bidding his officers wait his return and not be drawn from their position before he came again to them; and taking some of his younger knights and a few more, he passed out of his camp, and paused for a moment, bidding those with him spread themselves out in a thin line, in order the better to reconnoitre, and that, if some fell into an ambuscade, others might survive to carry the news back to the camp. And he, having given his order, himself stood resting on his sword. But in an instant, before he could so much as lift the point of his sword from the ground, silent blurred shapes came from the mist,

and were in front and behind and round him;
and they looked so strange that he raised his
hand to cross himself; but then a scarf was
thrown over his mouth, and he was seized by
eight strong hands and held so that he could not
struggle; and neither could he cry out by reason
of the scarf across his mouth. And they that
held him began to run rapidly; and he was
carried out of the camp without the knowledge
of any of those who were with him, and they,
missing their leader, fell presently into a great
consternation, and ran to and fro in the gloom
crying, "The Prince? Have you seen the
Prince? Is His Highness with you? In God's
name, has the Prince been this way?" But they
did not find him, and they grew more con-
founded, stumbling against one another and
being much afraid. And when the Prince was
nowhere to be found, they lost heart, and began to fall back towards their own borders,
skirting the base of Agnino. And their retreat grew quicker; and at last, when morning came, they were near the border; but the
fog still wrapped all the plain in obscurity,

and, robbed of their leader, they dared attempt nothing.

Now the Prince of Mantivoglia, whom his army sought thus in fear and bewilderment, was carried very quickly up to the high ground, where the rocks grew steep and close and the way led to the peak of Agnino. And as he was borne along, some one bound his hands and his feet; and still he was carried up, till at last he found himself laid down gently on the ground. And though he knew no fear—for they of Mantivoglia have ever been most valiant Princes and strangers to all fear—yet he thought that his last hour was come, and, fearing God though he feared nothing else, he said a prayer and commended his soul to the Almighty, grieving that he should not receive the last services of the Church. And having done this, he lay still until the dawning day smote on his eyes and he could see; for the fog that lay dense on the plain was not in the hills, but hung between them and the plain. And he looked round, but saw no man. So he abode another hour, and then he heard a step behind him, and a man came, but whence he could not see; and the man stooped and loosed the scarf from his mouth and cut his bonds, and he sat up, uttering a cry of wonder. For Count Antonio stood before him, his sword sheathed by his side. And he said to the Prince of Mantivoglia, "Do to me what you will, my lord. If you will strike me as I stand, strike. Or if you will do me the honour to cross swords, my sword is ready. Or, my lord, if you will depart in peace and in my great love and reverence, I will give thanks to Heaven and to a noble Prince."

"Antonio, what does this mean?" cried the Prince, divided between anger and wonder.

Then Antonio told him all that he had done: how the Duke was gone back with his army to Firmola, and how the Prince's army had retreated towards the borders of Mantivoglia; for of all this his men had informed him; and he ended, saying, "For since it seemed that I was to be the most unworthy cause of more fighting between two great Princes, it came into my head that such a thing should not be. And I rejoice that now it will not; for the townsmen will not march out again this year at least, and Your

Highness will scarce sit down before Firmola with the season now far gone."

"So I am baulked?" cried the Prince, and he rose to his feet. "And this trick is played me by a friend!"

"I am of Firmola," said Antonio, flushing red. "And while there was war, I might in all honour have played another trick, and carried you not hither, but to Firmola."

"I care not," cried the Prince angrily. "It was a trick, and no fair fighting."

"Be it as you will, my lord," said Antonio. "A man's own conscience is his only judge. Will you draw your sword, my lord?"

But the Prince was very angry, and he answered roughly, "I will not fight with you, and I will not speak more with you. I will go."

"I will lead Your Highness to your horse," said Antonio.

Then he led him some hundreds of paces down the hill, and they came where a fine horse stood ready saddled.

"It is not my horse," said the Prince.

"Be not afraid, my lord, It is not mine,

either," said Antonio smiling. "A rogue who serves me, and is called Bena, forgot his manners so far as to steal it from the quarters of the Duke. I pray you use some opportunity of sending it back to him, or I shall be dubbed horse-stealer with the rest."

"I am glad it is not yours," said the Prince, and he prepared to mount, Antonio holding the stirrup for him. And when he was mounted, Antonio told him how to ride, so that he should come safely to his own men, and avoid certain scouting parties of the Duke that he had thrown out behind him as he marched back to Firmola. And having done this, Antonio stood back and bared his head and bowed.

"And where is your horse?" asked the Prince suddenly.

"I have no horse, my lord," said Antonio. "My men with all my horses have ridden back to our hiding-place in the hills. I am alone here, for I thought that Your Highness would kill me, and I should need no horse."

"How, then, will you escape the scouting parties?"

"I fear I shall not escape them, my lord," said Antonio, smiling again.

"And if they take you?"

"Of a surety I shall be hanged," said Count Antonio.

The Prince of Mantivoglia gathered his brow into a heavy frown, but the corners of his lips twitched, and he did not look at Antonio. And thus they rested a few moments, till suddenly the Prince, unable to hold himself longer, burst into a great and merry peal of laughter; and he raised his fist and shook it at Antonio, crying, "A scurvy trick, Antonio! By my faith, a scurvier trick by far than that other of yours! Art thou not ashamed, man? Ah, you cast down your eyes! You dare not look at me, Antonio."

"Indeed I have naught to say for this last trick, my lord," said Antonio, laughing also.

"Indeed I must carry this knave with me!" cried the Prince. "Faugh, the traitor! Get up behind me, traitor! Clasp me by the waist, knave! Closer, knave! Ah, Antonio, I know not in what mood Heaven was when you were made! I would I had the heart to leave you to your hanging! For what a story will my Princess make of this! I shall be the best-derided man in all Mantivoglia."

"I think not, my dear lord," said Count Antonio, "unless a love that a man may reckon on as his lady-love's and a chivalry that does not fail, and a valour that has set two armies all agape in wonder, be your matters for mirth in Mantivoglia. And indeed, my lord, I would that I were riding to the lady I love best in the world, as Your Highness rides; for she might laugh till her sweet eyes ran tears so I were near to dry them."

The Prince put back his hand towards Antonio and clasped Antonio's hand, and said, "What said she when you left her, Antonio? For with women love is often more than honour, and their tears rust the bright edge of a man's conscience."

"Her heart is even as Our Lady's, and with tears and smiles she left me," said Antonio, and he grasped the Prince's hand. "Come, my lord, we must ride, or it is a prison for you and a halter for me."

So they rode together in the morning on the horse that Bena had stolen from among the choicest of Duke Valentine's, and, keeping cunningly among the spurs of the hills, they were sighted once only from afar off by the Duke's scouts, and escaped at a canter, and came safe to the Prince's army, where they were received with great wonder and joy. But the Prince would not turn again to besiege Firmola, for he had had a fill of fighting, and the season grew late for the siege of a walled town. So he returned with all his force to Mantivoglia, having won by his expedition much praise of valour, and nothing else in the wide world besides; which thing indeed is so common in the wars of princes that even wise men have well-nigh ceased to wonder at it.

But the Princess of Mantivoglia heard all that had passed with great mirth, and made many jests upon her husband; and again, lest the Prince should take her jesting in evil part, more upon Duke Valentine. But concerning Count Antonio and the Lady Lucia she did not jest. Yet one day, chancing to be alone with Count

Antonio—for he stayed many days at the Court of Mantivoglia, and was treated with great honour—she said to him, with a smile and half-raised eyelids, "Had I been a man, my lord Antonio, I would not have returned alone from the gates of Firmola. In truth, your lady needs patience for her virtue, Count Antonio!"

"I trust, then, that Heaven sends it to her, madame," said Antonio.

"And to you also," she retorted with a laugh. "And to her trust in you also, I pray. For an absent lover is often an absent heart, Antonio, and I hear that many ladies would fain soften your exile. And what I hear, the Lady Lucia may hear also."

"She would hear it as the idle babbling of water over stones," said Antonio. "But, madame, I am glad that I have some honesty in me. For if there were not honest men and true maids in this world, I think more than a half of the wits would starve for lack of food."

"Mercy, mercy!" she cried. "Indeed your wit has a keen edge, my lord."

"Yet it is not whetted on truth and honesty," said he.

She answered nothing for a moment; then she drew near to him and stood before him, regarding his face; and she sighed "Heigh-ho!" and again "Heigh-ho!" and dropped her eyes, and raised them again to his face; and at last she said, "To some faithfulness is easy. I give no great praise to the Lady Lucia." And when she had said this she turned and left him, and was but little more in his company so long as he stayed at Mantivoglia. And she spoke no more of the Lady Lucia. But when he was mounting, after bidding her farewell, she gave him a white rose from her bosom, saying carelessly, "Your colour, my lord, and the best. Yet God made the other roses also."

"All that He made He loves, and in all there is good," said Antonio, and he bowed very low, and, having kissed her hand, took the rose; and he looked into her eyes and smiled, saying, "Heaven give peace where it has given wit and beauty;" and so he rode away to join his company in the hills. And the Princess of Mantivoglia, having watched till he was out of sight, went into dinner, and was merrier than ever she had shown herself before; so that they said, "She feared Antonio and is glad that he is gone." Yet that night, while her husband slept, she wept.

CHAPTER IV.

COUNT ANTONIO AND THE WIZARD'S DRUG.

THE opinion of man is ever in flux save where it is founded on the rock of true religion. What our fathers believed, we disbelieve; but often our sons shall again receive it. In olden time men held much by magic and black arts; now such are less esteemed; yet hereafter it may well be that the world will find new incantations and fresh spells, the same impulse flowing in a different channel and never utterly to be checked or stemmed by the censures of the Church or the mocking of unbelievers. As for truth—in truth who knows truth? For the light of Revelation shines but in few places, and for the rest we are in natural darkness, groping along unseen paths towards unknown ends. May God keep our footsteps!

Now towards the close of the third year of his outlawry the heart of Count Antonio of Monte Velluto had grown very sad. For it was above the space of a year since he had heard news of the Lady Lucia, and hard upon two since he had seen her face; so closely did Duke Valentine hold her prisoner in Firmola. And as he walked to and fro among his men in their hiding place in the hills, his face was sorrowful. Yet, coming where Tommasino and Bena sat together, he stopped and listened to their talk with a smile. For Bena cried to Tommasino, "By the saints, my lord, it is even so! My father himself had a philtre from him thirty years ago; and though, before, my mother had loathed to look on my father, yet now here am I, nine-and-twenty years of age and a child born in holy wedlock. Never tell me that it is foolishness, my lord!"

"Of whom do you speak, Bena?" asked Antonio.

"Of the Wizard of Baratesta, my lord. Aye, and he can do more than make a love-potion. He can show you all that shall come to you in a mirror, and make the girl you love rise before your eyes as though the shape were good flesh and blood."

"All this is foolishness, Bena," said Count Antonio.

"Well, God knows that," said Bena. "But he did it for my father; and as he is thirty years older, he will be wiser still by now;" and Bena strode off to tend his horse, somewhat angry that Antonio paid so little heed to his words.

"It is all foolishness, Tommasino," said Antonio.

"They say that of many a thing which gives a man pleasure," said Tommasino.

"I have heard of this man before," continued the Count, "and marvellous stories are told of him. Now I leave what shall come to me in the hands of Heaven; for to know is not to alter, and knowledge without power is but fretting of the heart; but——" And Antonio broke off.

"Ride then, if you can safely, and beg him to show you Lucia's face," said Tommasino. "For to that I think you are making."

"In truth I was, fool that I am," said Antonio.

"But be wary; for Baratesta is but ten miles from the city, and His Highness sleeps with an open eye."

So Antonio, albeit that he was in part ashamed, learnt from Bena where the wizard dwelt on the bridge that is outside the gate of Baratesta—for the Syndic would not suffer such folk to live inside the wall—and one evening he saddled his horse and rode alone to seek the wizard, leaving Tommasino in charge of the band. And as he went, he pondered, saying, "I am a fool, yet I would see her face;" and thus, still dubbing himself fool, yet still persisting, he came to the bridge of Baratesta; and the wizard, who was a very old man and tall and marvellously lean, met him at the door of the house, crying, "I looked for your coming, my lord." And he took Antonio's horse from him and stood it in a stable beside the house, and led Antonio in, saying again, "Your coming was known to me, my lord;" and he brought Antonio to a chamber at the back of the house, having one window, past which the river, being then in flood, rushed with noise and fury. There were many strange things in the chamber, skulls and the forms of animals from far-off countries, great jars, basins, and retorts, and in one corner a mirror half-draped in a black cloth.

"You know who I am?" asked Antonio.

"That needs no art," answered the wizard, "and I pretend to none in it. Your face, my lord, was known to me as to any other man, from seeing you ride with the Duke before your banishment."

"And you knew that I rode hither to-night?"

"Aye," said the wizard. "For the stars told of the coming of some great man; and I turned from my toil and watched for you."

"What toil?" asked Antonio. "See, here is money, and I have a quiet tongue. What toil?"

The wizard pointed to a heap of broken and bent pieces of base metal. "I was turning dross to gold," said he, in a fearful whisper.

"Can you do that?" asked Antonio, smiling.

"I can, my lord, though but slowly."

"And hate to love?" asked Count Antonio.

The wizard laughed harshly. "Let them that prize love, seek that," said he. "It is not for me."

"I would it had been; then had my errand here been a better one. For I am come to see the semblance of a maiden's face."

The wizard frowned as he said, "I had looked for a greater matter. For you have a mighty enemy, my lord, and I have means of power for freeing men of their enemies."

But Count Antonio, knowing that he spoke of some dark device of spell or poison, answered, "Enough! enough! For I am a man of quick temper, and it is not well to tell me of wicked things, lest I be tempted to anticipate Heaven's punishment."

"I shall not die at your hands, my lord," said the wizard. "Come, will you see what shall befall you?"

"Nay, I would but see my lady's face; a great yearning for that has come over me, and, although I take shame in it, yet it has brought me here."

"You shall see it then; and if you see more,

it is not by my will," said the wizard; and he quenched the lamp that burned on the table, and flung a handful of some powder on the charcoal in the stove; and the room was filled with a thick sweet-smelling vapour. And the wizard tore the black cloth off the face of the mirror and bade Antonio look steadily in the mirror. Antonio looked till the vapour that enveloped all the room cleared off from the face of the mirror, and the wizard, laying his hand on Antonio's shoulder, said, "Cry her name thrice." And Antonio thrice cried "Lucia!" and again waited. Then something came on the polished surface of the mirror; but the wizard muttered low and angrily, for it was not the form of Lucia nor of any maiden; yet presently he cried low, "Look, my lord, look!" and Antonio, looking, saw a dim, and shadowy face in the mirror; and the wizard began to fling his body to and fro, uttering strange whispered words; and the sweat stood in beads on his forehead. "Now, now!" he cried; and Antonio, with beating heart, fastened his gaze on the mirror. And as the story goes (I vouch not for it) he saw, though very dimly, the face of Lucia; but more he saw also; for beside the face was his own face, and there was a rope about his neck, and the half-shaped arm of a gibbet seemed to hover above him. And he shrank back for an instant.

"What more you see is not by my will," said the wizard.

"What shall come is only by God's will," said Antonio. "I have seen her face. It is enough."

But the wizard clutched him by the arm, whispering in terror, "It is a gibbet; and the rope is about your neck."

"Indeed, I seem to have worn it there these three years, and it is not drawn tight yet; nor is it drawn in the mirror."

"You have a good courage," said the wizard with a grim smile. "I will show you more;" and he flung another powder on the charcoal; and the shapes passed from the mirror. But another came; and the wizard, with a great cry, fell suddenly on his knees, exclaiming, "They mock me, they mock me! They show what they will, not what I will. Ah, my lord, whose is the face in the mirror?" And he seized Antonio again by the arm.

"It is your face," said Antonio; "and it is the face of a dead man, for his jaw has dropped, and his features are drawn and wrung."

The wizard buried his face in his hands; and so they rested awhile till the glass of the mirror cleared; and Antonio felt the body of the wizard shaking against his knee.

"You are old," said Antonio, "and death must come to all. Maybe it is a lie of the devil; but if not, face it as a man should."

But the wizard trembled still; and Antonio, casting a pitiful glance on him, rose to depart. But on the instant as he moved, there came a sudden loud knocking at the door of the house, and he stood still. The wizard lifted his head to listen.

"Have you had warning of more visitors tonight?" asked Antonio.

"I know not what happens to-night," muttered the wizard. "My power is gone to-night."

The knocking at the door came again, loud and impatient.

"They will beat the door down if you do not open," said Antonio. "I will hide myself here behind the mirror; for I cannot pass them without being seen; and if I am seen here, it is like enough that the mirror will be proved right both for you and me."

So Antonio hid himself, crouching down behind the mirror; and the wizard, having lit a small dim lamp, went on trembling feet to the door. And presently he came back, followed by two men whose faces were hid in their cloaks. One of them sat down, but the other stood and flung his cloak back over his shoulders; and Antonio, observing him from behind the mirror, saw that he was Lorenzo, the Duke's favourite.

Then Lorenzo spoke to the wizard saying, "Why did you not come sooner to open the door?"

"There was one here with me," said the wizard, whose air had become again composed.

"And is he gone? For we would be alone."

"He is not to be seen," answered the wizard. "Utterly alone here you cannot be."

When he heard this, Lorenzo turned pale, for

he did not love this midnight errand to the wizard's chamber.

"But no man is here," said the wizard.

A low hoarse laugh came from the man who sat. "Tricks of the trade, tricks of the trade!" said he; and Antonio started to hear his voice. "Be sure that where a prince, a courtier, and a cheat are together, the devil makes a fourth. But there is no need to turn pale over it, Lorenzo."

When the wizard heard, he fell on his knees; for he knew that it was Duke Valentine who spoke.

"Look you, fellow," pursued His Highness, "you owe me much thanks that you are not hanged already; for by putting an end to you I should please my clergy much and the Syndic of Baratesta not a little. But if you do not obey me to-night, you shall be dead before morning."

"I shall not die unless it be written in the stars," said the wizard, but his voice trembled.

"I know nothing of the stars," said the Duke, "but I know the mind of the Duke of Firmola, and that is enough for my purpose." And he rose and began to walk about the chamber, examining the strange objects that were there; and thus he came in front of the mirror, and stood within half a yard of Antonio. But Lorenzo stood where he was, and once he crossed himself secretly and unobserved.

"What would my lord the Duke?" asked the wizard.

"There is a certain drug," said the Duke, turning round towards the wizard, "which if a man drink—or a woman, Lorenzo—he can walk on his legs and use his arms, and seem to be waking and in his right mind; yet is his mind a nothing, for he knows not what he does, but does everything that one, being with him, may command, and without seeming reluctance; and again, when bidden, he will seem to lose all power of movement, and to lack his senses. I saw the thing once when I sojourned with the Lord of Florence; for a wizard there, having given the drug to a certain man, put him through strange antics, and he performed them all willingly."

"Aye, there is such a drug," said the wizard.

"Then give it me," said the Duke; "and I give you your life and fifty pieces of gold. For I have great need of it."

Now when Antonio heard the Duke's words, he was seized with great fear; for he surmised that it was against Lucia that the Duke meant to use this drug; and noiselessly he loosened his sword in its sheath and bent forward again to listen.

"And though my purpose is nothing to you, yet it is a benevolent purpose. Is it not, Lorenzo?"

"It is your will, not mine, my lord," said Lorenzo in a troubled voice.

"Mine shall be the crime, then, and yours the reward," laughed the Duke. "For I will give her the drug, and she shall wed you."

Then Antonio doubted no longer of what was afoot, nor that a plot was laid whereby Lucia should be entrapped into marriage with Lorenzo, since she could not be openly forced. And anger burned hotly in him. And he swore that, sooner than suffer the thing to be done, he would kill the Duke there with his own hand or himself be slain.

"And you alone know of this drug now, they say," the Duke went on. "For the wizard of Florence is dead. Therefore give it me quickly."

But the wizard answered, "It will not serve, my lord, that I give you the drug. With my own hand I must give it to the persons whom you would thus affect, and I must tell them what they should do."

"More tricks!" said the Duke scornfully. "I know your ways. Give me the drug." And he would not believe what the wizard said.

"It is even as I say," said the wizard. "And if Your Highness will carry the drug yourself, I will not vouch its operation."

"Give it me; for I know the appearance of it," said the Duke.

Then the wizard, having again protested, went to a certain shelf and from some hidden recess took a small phial, and came with it to the Duke, saying, "Blame me not, if its operation fail."

The Duke examined the phial closely, and

also smelt its smell. "It is the same," said he. "It will do its work."

Then Count Antonio, who believed no more than the Duke what the wizard had said concerning the need of his own presence for the working of the drug, was very sorely put to it to stay quietly where he was; for if the Duke rode away now with the phial, he might well find means to give it to the Lady Lucia before any warning could be conveyed to her. And, although the danger was great, yet his love for Lucia and his fear for her overcame his prudence, and suddenly he sprang from behind the mirror, drawing his sword and crying, "Give me that drug, my lord, or your life must answer for it."

But fortune served him ill; for as the Duke and Lorenzo shrank back at his sudden appearance, and he was about to spring on them, behold, his foot caught in the folds of the black cloth that had been over the mirror and now lay on the ground, and, falling forward, he struck his head on the marble rim that ran round the charcoal stove, and, having fallen with great force, lay there like a man dead. With loud cries of triumph, the Duke and Lorenzo, having drawn their swords, ran upon him; and the Duke planted his foot upon his neck, crying, "Heaven sends a greater prize! At last, at last I have him! Bind his hands, Lorenzo."

Lorenzo bound Antonio's hands as he lay there, a log for stillness. The Duke turned to the wizard and a smile bent his lips. "O faithful subject and servant!" said he. "Well do you requite my mercy and forbearance, by harbouring my bitterest enemies and suffering them to hear my secret counsels. Had not Antonio chanced to trip, it is like enough he would have slain Lorenzo and me also. What shall be your reward, O faithful servant?"

When the Wizard of Baratesta beheld the look that was on Duke Valentine's face, he suddenly cried aloud, "The mirror, the mirror!" and sank in a heap on the floor, trembling in every limb; for he remembered the aspect of his own face in the mirror and knew that the hour of his death had come. And he feared mightily to die; therefore he besought the Duke very piteously, and told him again that from his hand alone could the drug receive its potency. And so earnest was he in this, that at last he half-won upon the Duke, so that the Duke wavered. And as he doubted, his eye fell on Antonio; and he perceived that Antonio was recovering from his swoon.

"There is enough for two," said he, "in the phial; and we will put this thing to the test. But if you speak or move or make any sign, forthwith in that moment you shall die." Then the Duke poured half the contents of the phial into a glass and came to Lorenzo and whispered to him, "If the drug works on him, and the wizard is proved to lie, the wizard shall die; but we will carry Antonio with us; and when I have mustered my Guard, I will hang him in the square as I have sworn. But if the drug does not work, then we must kill him here; for I fear to carry him against his will; for he is a wonderful man, full of resource, and the people also love him. Therefore, if the operation of the drug fail, run him through with your sword when I give the signal."

Now Antonio was recovering from his swoon,

and he overheard part of what the Duke said, but not all. As to the death of the wizard he did not hear, but he understood that the Duke was about to test the effect of the drug on him, and that if it had no effect, he was to die; whereas, if its operation proved sufficient, he should go alive; and he saw here a chance for his life in case what the wizard had said should prove true.

"Drink, Antonio," said the Duke softly. "No harm comes to you. Drink: it is a refreshing draught."

And Antonio drank the draught, the wizard looking on with parted lips and with great drops of sweat running from his forehead and thence down his cheeks to his mouth, so that his lips were salt when he licked them. And the Duke, having seen that Lorenzo had his sword ready for Antonio, took his stand by the wizard with the dagger from his belt in his hand. And he cried to Antonio, "Rise." And Antonio rose up. The wizard started a step towards him; but the Duke showed his dagger, and said to Antonio, "Will you go with me to Firmola, Antonio?"

And Antonio answered, "I will go."

"Do you love me, Antonio?" asked the Duke.

"Aye, my lord," answered Antonio.

"Yet you have done many wicked things against me."

"True, my lord," said Antonio.

"Is your mind then changed?"

"It is, my lord," said Antonio.

"Then leap two paces into the air," said the Duke; and Antonio straightway obeyed.

"Go down on your knees and crawl;" and Antonio crawled, smiling secretly to himself.

Then the Duke bade Lorenzo mount Antonio on his horse; and he commanded the wizard to follow him; and they all went out where the horses were; and the three mounted, and the wizard followed; and they came to the end of the bridge. There the Duke turned sharp round and rode by the side of the rushing river. And, suddenly pausing, he said to Antonio, "Commend thy soul to God and leap in."

And Antonio commended his soul to God, and would have leapt in; but the Duke caught him by the arm even as he set spurs to his horse, saying, "Do not leap." And Antonio stayed his leap. Then the Duke turned his face on the wizard, saying, "The potion works, wizard. Why did you lie?"

Then the wizard fell on his knees, cursing hell and heaven; for he could not see how he should escape. For the potion worked. And Antonio wondered what should fall out next. But Duke Valentine leapt down from his horse and approached the wizard, while Lorenzo set his sword against Antonio's breast. And the Duke, desirous to make a final trial, cried again to Antonio, "Fling yourself from your horse." And Antonio, having his arms bound, yet flung himself from his horse, and fell prone on the ground, and lay there sorely bruised.

"It is enough," said the Duke. "You lied, wizard."

But the wizard cried, "I lied not, I lied not, my lord. Slay me not, my lord! For I dare not die."

But the Duke caught him by the throat and drove his dagger into his breast till the fingers that held the dagger were buried in the folds of the wizard's doublet; and the Duke pulled out the dagger, and, when the wizard fell, he pushed him with his foot over the brink, and the body fell with a loud splash into the river below.

Thus died the Wizard of Baratesta, who was famed above all of his day for the hidden knowledge that he had; yet he served not God, but Satan, and his end was the end of a sinner. And, many days after, his body was found a hundred miles from that place; and certain charitable men, brethren of my own order, gave it burial. So that he died that same night in which the mirror had shown him his face as the face of a dead man; but whence came the vision I know not.

Then the Duke set Antonio again on his horse, and the three rode together towards Firmola, and as they went, again and again the Duke tested the operation of the drug, setting Antonio many strange, ludicrous, and unseemly things to do and to say; and Antonio did and said them all. But he wondered greatly that the drug had no power over him, and that his brain was clear and his senses all his own; nor did he then believe that the Duke had, in truth, slain the wizard for any reason save that the wizard had harboured him, an outlaw, and suffered him to hear the Duke's counsels: and he was grieved at the wizard's death.

Thus they rode through the night; and it was the hour of dawn when they came to the gates of Firmola. Now Antonio was puzzled what he should do; for having been in a swoon, he knew not whether the Duke had more of the potion; nor could he tell with certainty whether the potion would be powerless against the senses of a weak girl as it had proved against his own. Therefore he said to the Duke, "I pray you, my lord, give me more of that sweet drink. For it has refreshed me and set my mind at rest from all trouble."

"Nay, Antonio, you have had enough," said the Duke, bantering him. "I have another use for the rest." And they were now nearing the gates of Firmola. Then Antonio began to moan pitifully, saying, "These bonds hurt my hands;" and he whined and did as a child would do, feigning to cry. The Duke laughed in bitter triumph, saying to Lorenzo, "Indeed it is a princely drug that makes Antonio of Monte Velluto like a peevish child!" And being now very secure of the power of the drug, he bade Lorenzo loosen the bonds, saying to Antonio, "Take the reins, Antonio, and ride with us into the city."

And Antonio answered, "I will, my good lord."

"It is even as I saw when I was with the Lord of Florence," whispered the Duke in exultation.

"Yet I will still have my sword ready," said Lorenzo.

"There is no need; he is like a tame dog," said the Duke carelessly.

But the Duke was not minded to produce Antonio to the people till all his Guards were collected and under arms, and the people thus restrained by a great show of force. Therefore he bade Antonio cover his face with his cloak; and Antonio, Lorenzo's sword being still at his breast, obeyed; and thus they three rode through the gates of Firmola and came to the Duke's palace; and Antonio did all that the Duke ordered, and babbled foolishly like a bewildered child when the Duke asked him questions, so that His Highness laughed mightily, and, coming into the garden, sat down in his favourite place by the fish-pond, causing Antonio to stand over against him.

"Indeed, Antonio," said he, "I can do no other than hang you."

"If it be your pleasure, my lord."

"And then Lucia shall drink of this wonderful drug also, and she will be content and obedient, and will gladly wed Lorenzo. Let us have her here now, and give it to her without delay. You do not fret at that, Antonio? You love not the obstinate girl?"

"In truth, no," laughed Antonio. "She is naught to me!" And he put his hand to his head, saying perplexedly, "Lucia? Yes, I remember that name. Who was she? Was she aught to me, my lord?"

Then Lorenzo wondered greatly, and the doubts that he had held concerning the power of the wizard's drug melted away; yet he did not laugh like the Duke, but looked on Antonio and said sadly to the Duke, sinking his voice, "Not thus should Antonio of Monte Velluto have died."

"So he dies, I care not how," answered the Duke. "Indeed, I love to see him a witless fool even while his body is yet alive. O rare wizard, I go near to repenting having done justice on you! Go, Lorenzo, to the officer of the Guard and bid him fetch hither the Lady Lucia, and we will play the pretty comedy to the end."

"Will you be alone with him?" asked Lorenzo.

"Aye; why not? See! he is tame enough," and he buffeted Antonio in the face with his riding-glove. And Antonio whimpered and whined.

Now the officer of the Guard was in his lodge at the entrance of the palace, on the other side of the great hall; and Lorenzo turned and went, and presently the sound of his feet on the marble floor of the hall grew faint and distant. The Duke sat with the phial in his hand, smiling at Antonio who crouched at his feet. And Antonio drew himself on his knees quite close to the

Duke, and looked up in his face with a foolish empty smile. And the Duke, laughing, buffeted him again. Then, with a sudden spring, like the spring of that Indian tiger which the Mogul of Delhi sent lately as a gift to the Most Christian King, and the king, for his diversion, made to slay deer before him at the *château* of Blois (which I myself saw, being there on a certain mission, and wonderful was the sight), Count Antonio, leaping, was upon the Duke; and he snatched the philtre from the Duke's hand and seized the Duke's head in his hands and wrenched his jaw open, and he poured the contents of the phial down the Duke's throat, and the Duke swallowed the potion. Then Antonio fixed a stern and imperious glance on the Duke, nailing his eyes to the Duke's and the Duke's to his, and he said in a voice of command, "Obey! You have drunk the potion!" And still he kept his eyes on the Duke's. And the Duke, amazed, suddenly began to tremble, and sought to rise; and Antonio took his hands off him, but said, "Sit there, and move not." Then, although Antonio's hands were no longer upon him, yet His Highness did not rise, but after a short struggle with himself sank back in his seat, and stared at Antonio like a bird fascinated by a snake. And he moaned, "Take away your eyes; they burn my brain. Take them away." But Antonio gazed all the more intently at him, saying, "Be still, be still!" and holding up his arm in enforcement of his command. And Antonio took from the Duke the sword that he wore and the dagger wherewith the Duke had killed the Wizard of Baratesta, he making no resistance, but sitting motionless with bewildered stare. Then Antonio looked round, for he knew that Lorenzo would soon come. And for the last time he bent his eyes again on the Duke's eyes in a very long gaze and the Duke cowered and shivered, moaning, "You hurt me, you hurt me."

Then Antonio said, "Be still and speak not till I return and bid you;" and he suddenly left the Duke and ran at the top of his speed along under the wall of the garden, and came where the wall ended; and there was a flight of steps leading up on to the top of the wall. Running up it, Antonio stood for a moment on the wall; and the river ran fifty feet below. But he heard a cry from the garden, and beheld Lorenzo rushing up to the Duke, and behind Lorenzo, the Captain of the Guard and, two men who led a maiden in white. Then Count Antonio, having commended himself to the keeping of God, leapt head foremost from the top of the wall into the river, and his body clove the water as an arrow cleaves the wand.

Now Lorenzo marvelled greatly at what he saw, and came to the Duke crying, "My lord, what does this mean? Antonio flies!" But the Duke answered nothing, sitting with empty eyes and lips set in a rigid smile; nor did he move. "My lord, what ails you?" cried Lorenzo. Yet the Duke did not answer. Then Lorenzo's eye fell on the fragments of the phial which lay broken on the rim of the fish-pond where Antonio had flung it; and he cried out in great alarm, "The potion! Where is the potion?" But the Duke did not answer. And Lorenzo was much bewildered and in sore fear; for it seemed as though His Highness's senses were gone; and Lorenzo said, "By some means he has drunk the potion!" And he ran up to the Duke, and caught him by the arm and shook him violently, seeking to rouse him from his stupor, and calling his name with entreaties, and crying, "He escapes, my lord; Antonio escapes! Rouse yourself, my lord—he escapes!" But the Duke did no more than lift heavy dull eyes to Lorenzo's face in puzzled inquiry.

And, seeing the strange thing, the Captain of the Guard hurried up, and with him the Lady Lucia, and she said, "Alas, my lord is ill!" and coming to His Highness she set her cool soft hand on his hot throbbing brow, and took perfume from a silver flask that hung at her girdle, and wetted her handkerchief with it and bathed his brow, whispering soft soothing words to him, as though he had been a sick woman. For let a woman have what grudge she may against a man, yet he gains pardon for all so soon as he becomes sick enough to let her nurse and comfort him; and Lucia was as tender to the Duke as to the Count Antonio himself, and forgot all save the need of giving him ease and rousing him from his stupor.

But Lorenzo cried angrily, "I at least have my senses!" And he said to the Captain of the Guard, "I must needs stay with His Highness; but Antonio of Monte Velluto has leapt from the wall into the river. Go and bring him here, dead or alive, and I will be your warrant to the Duke. But if he be as when I saw him last, he will give you small trouble. For he was like a child for weakness and folly." And having said this, he turned to the Duke again, and gave his aid to Lucia's ministrations.

Now the gentleman who commanded the Duke's Guard at this time was a Spaniard, by name Corogna, and he was young, of high courage, and burning to do some great deed. Therefore he said, "I pray he be as he is wont to be: yet I will bring him to the feet of my lord the Duke." And he ran swiftly through the hall and called for his horse, and drawing his sword, rode alone out of the city and across the bridge, seeking Antonio, and saying to himself, "What a thing if I take him! And if he slay me, why, I will show that a gentleman of Andalusia can die;" yet he thought for an instant of the house where his mother lived. Then he scanned the plain, and he beheld a man running some half-mile away; and the man seemed to be making for the hill on which stood the ruins of Antonio's house that the Duke had burnt. Then Corogna set spurs to his horse; but the man, whom by his stature and gait Corogna knew to be Antonio, ran very swiftly, and was not overtaken before he came to the hill; and he began to mount by a very steep rugged path, and he was out of sight in the trees when Corogna came to the foot. And Corogna's horse stumbled among the stones, and could not mount the path; so Corogna sprang off his back and ran on foot up the path, sword in hand. And he came in sight of Antonio round a curve of the path three parts of the way up the hill. Antonio was leaning against the trunk of a tree and wringing the water out of his cloak. Corogna drew near, sword in hand, and with a prayer to the Holy Virgin on his lips. And he trembled, not with fear, but because fate offered a great prize, and his name would be famed throughout Italy if he slew or took Antonio of Monte Velluto; and for fame, even as for a woman's smile, a young man will tremble as a coward quakes with fear.

The Count Antonio stood as though sunk in a reverie; yet, presently, hearing Corogna's tread, he raised his eyes, and smiling kindly on the young man, he said, "Very strange are the ways of Heaven, sir. I think that the Wizard of Baratesta spoke truth, and did not lie to the Duke. Yet I had that same power which the wizard claimed, although the Duke had none over me. We are children, sir, and our game is blind-man's buff; but all are blinded, and it is but the narrowest glimpse that we obtain now and again by some clever shifting of the handkerchief. Yet there are some things clear enough; as that a man should do his work, and be clean and true. What would you with me, sir? For I do not think I know you."

"I am of Andalusia, and my name is Corogna. I am Captain of His Highness's Guard, and I come to bring you, alive or dead, to his presence."

"And are you come alone on that errand, sir?" asked Antonio with a smile that he strove to smother, lest it should wound the young man's honour.

"David slew Goliath, my lord," said the Spaniard with a bow.

Then Count Antonio held out his hand to the young man and said courteously, "Sir, your valour needs no proof and fears no reproach. I pray you suffer me to go in peace. I would not fight with you, if I may avoid it honourably. For what has happened has left me more in the mood for thinking than for fighting. Besides, sir, you are young, and, far off in Andalusia, loving eyes, and maybe sparkling eyes, are strained to the horizon, seeking your face as you return."

"What is all that, my lord?" asked Corogna. "I am a man, though a young one; and I am here to carry you to the Duke." And he touched Antonio's sword with his, saying, "Guard yourself."

"It is with great pain and reluctance that I take my sword, and I call you to witness of it;

but if I must, I must;" and the Count took up his position and they crossed swords.

Now Corogna was well-taught and skilful, but he did not know the cunning which Antonio had learned in the school of Giacomo in Padua, nor had he the strength and endurance of the Count. Antonio would fain have wearied him out, and then, giving him some slight wound to cover his honour, have left him and escaped; but the young man came at him impetuously, and neglected to guard himself while he thrust at his enemy: once and again the Count spared him; but he did not know that he had received the courtesy, and taking heart from his immunity came at Antonio more fiercely again; until at last Antonio, breathing a sigh, stiffened his arm, and, waiting warily for the young man again to uncover himself, thrust at his breast, and the sword's point entered hard by the young man's heart; and the young man staggered, and would have fallen, dropping his sword; but Antonio cast away his own sword and supported him, stanching the blood from the wound and crying, "God send I have not killed him!"

And on his speech came the voice of Tommasino, saying carelessly, "Here, in truth, cousin, is a good prayer wasted on a Spaniard!"

Antonio, looking up, saw Tommasino and Bena. And Tommasino said, "When you did not come back, we set out to seek you, fearing that you were fallen into some snare and danger. And behold, we find you nursing this young spark; and how you missed his heart, Antonio, I know not, nor what Giacomo of Padua would say to such bungling."

But Antonio cared not for his cousin's words, which were spoken in a banter that a man uses to hide his true feelings; and they three set themselves to save the young man's life; for Tommasino and Bena had seen the better part of the fight and perceived that he was a gallant youth. But as they tended him, there came shouts and the sound of horses' hoofs mounting the hill by the winding road that led past Antonio's house. And Tommasino touched Antonio on the shoulder, saying, "We can do no more for him; and if we linger, we must fight again."

Then they laid the young man down, Antonio stripping off his cloak and making a pillow of it; and Bena brought the horses, for they had led one with them for Antonio, in case there should be need of it; and they were but just mounted when twenty of the Duke's Guard appeared three hundred yards away, ascending the crest of the hill.

"Thank Heaven there are so many," said Antonio, "for now we can flee without shame;" and they set spurs to their horses and fled. And certain of the Duke's Guard pursued, but only two or three were so well mounted as to be able to come near them; and these two or three, finding that they would be man to man, had no liking for the business, and each called out that his horse was foundered; and thus it was that none of them came up with Count Antonio, but all, after a while, returned together to the city, carrying the young Spaniard Corogna, their captain. But as they drew near to the gates, Corogna opened his eyes and murmured some soft-syllabled name that they could not hear, and, having with failing fingers signed the cross, turned on his side and died. And they brought his body to the great hall of the Duke's palace.

There in the great hall sat Duke Valentine: his face was pale and his frown heavy, and he gazed on the dead body of the young man and spoke no word. Yet he had loved Corogna, and out of love for him had made him Captain of his Guard. And he passed his hand wearily across his brow, murmuring, "I cannot think, I cannot think." And the Lady Lucia stood by him, her hand resting on his shoulder and her eyes full of tears. But at last the strange spell which lay on the senses of the Duke passed away: his eyes again had the light of reason in them, and he listened while they told him how Antonio had himself escaped, and had afterwards slain Corogna on the top of the hill where Antonio's house had stood. And the Duke was very sorry for Corogna's death: and he looked round on them all, saying, "He made of me a log of wood, and not a man. For when I had drunk and looked in his eyes, it seemed to me that my eyes were bound to his, and that I looked to him for command, and to know what

I should do, and that he was my God, and without his will I could not move. Yes, I was then to him even as he had seemed to be to me as we rode from Baratesta. And even now I am not free from this strange affection; for he seems still to be by me, and if his voice came now bidding me to do anything, by St. Prisian, I should arise and do it! Send my physician to me. And let this young man lie in the Chapel of the Blessed Virgin in the Cathedral, and to-morrow he shall be buried. But when I am well, and this strange affection is passed from me, and hangs no more like a fog over my brain, then I will exact the price of his death from Antonio, together with the reckoning of all else in respect of which he stands in my debt."

But the Lady Lucia, hearing this, said boldly, "My lord, it is by your deed and through your devices that this gentleman has met his death, and the blame of it is yours, and not my lord Antonio's."

At her bold and angry words Duke Valentine was roused, and the last of his languor left him; and he glared at her in wrath, crying

"Go to your house;" and he rose up suddenly from where he sat and went into his cabinet, Lorenzo attending him. And on the day after he walked first behind the bier of Corogna, and his face was very pale, but his air composed and his manner as it was wont to be. For the spell had passed and he was his own man again.

But Count Antonio heard with great grief of the death of the young man, and was very sorry that he had been constrained to kill him, and took great blame to himself for seeking counsel of the Wizard of Baratesta, whence had come death to the young man no less than to the wizard himself.

Such is the story of the drug which the Wizard of Baratesta gave to Duke Valentine of Firmola. To me it seems a strange tale, but yet it is well attested and stands on as strong a rock of testimony as anything which is told concerning the Count. The truth of it I do not understand, and often I ponder of it, wondering whether the Wizard of Baratesta spoke truth, and why the drug which had no power over

Count Antonio bound the senses and limbs of the Duke in utter torpor and helplessness. And once, when I was thus musing over the story, there came to my cell a monk of the Abbey of St. Prisian, who was an old man and very learned; and I went to walk with him in the garden, and coming to the fountain we sat down by the basin; and knowing that his lore was wide and deep, I set before him all the story, asking him if he knew of this strange drug; but he smiled at me, and taking the cup that lay by the basin of the fountain, he filled it with the clear sparkling water and drank a little, and held the cup to me, saying, "I think the Wizard of Baratesta would have wrought the spell as well with no other drug than this."

"You say a strange thing," said I.

"And I do not marvel," said he, "that the Duke had no power over Count Antonio, for he knew not how to wield such power. But neither do I wonder that power lay in Count Antonio to bend the mind of the Duke to his will. I warrant you, Ambrose, that the wonderful drug was not difficult to compound."

Then I understood what he meant; for he would have it that the drug was but a screen and a pretence, and that the power lay not in it, but in the man that gave it. Yet surely this is to explain what is obscure by a thing more obscure, and falls thus into a fault hated of the logicians. For Heaven may well have made a drug that binds the senses and limbs of men. Has not the poppy some such effect? And the ancients fabled the like of the lotus plant. But can we conceive that one man should by the mere glance of his eye have such power over another as to become to him, by these means and no other, a lord and master? In truth I find that hard to believe, and I doubt whether a man may lawfully believe it. Yet I know not. Knowledge spreads, and men grow wiser in hidden things; and although I who write may not live till the time when the thing shall be made clear, yet it may be God's will to send such light to the men of later days that, reading this story, they may find in it nothing that is strange or unknown to their science and skill. I pray that they may use the knowledge God sends in

His holy service, and not in the work of the devil, as did the Wizard of Baratesta.

But Count Antonio being, by his guile and adroitness, and by that strange power which he had from the drug or whence I know not, delivered out of the hands of Duke Valentine, abode with his company on the hills throughout the cold of winter, expecting the day when he might win the hand of the Lady Lucia; and she returned to her house, and said nothing of what had befallen the Duke. Yet the Duke showed her no tenderness, but rather used more severity with her. It is an evil service to a proud man to aid him in his day of humiliation.

CHAPTER V.

COUNT ANTONIO AND THE SACRED BONES.

THERE is one tale concerning Count Antonio of Monte Velluto, when he dwelt an outlaw in the hills, which men tell with fear and doubt, marvelling at the audacity of his act, and sometimes asking themselves whether he would in very truth have performed what he swore on the faith of his honour he would do, in case the Duke did not accede to his demands. For the thing he threatened was such as no man of Firmola dares think on without a shudder; for we of Firmola prize and reverence the bones of our saint, the holy martyr Prisian, above and far beyond every other relic, and they are to us as it were the sign and testimony of God's enduring favour to our country. But much will a man do for love of a woman, and Antonio's temper brooked no obstacle: so that I, who know all the truth of the matter, may not doubt that he would have done even as he said, braving the wrath of Heaven and making naught of the terror and consternation that had fallen on the city and the parts round about it. Whether that thought of his heart was such as would gain pardon, I know not: had the thing been done, I could scarce hope even in Heaven's infinite mercy. Yet this story also I must tell, lest I be charged with covering up what shames Antonio; for with the opinions of careless and faithless men (who are too many in this later age) I have no communion, and I tell the tale not to move laughter or loose jests, but rather that I may show to what extremity a man in nature good may be driven by harshness and the unmerited disfavour of his Prince.

In the third year, then, of Count Antonio's outlawry, His Highness the Duke looked on the Lady Lucia and found that she was of full age for marriage. Therefore he resolved that she should be wed, and, since Robert de Beauregard, to whom he had purposed to give her, was dead, he chose from among his lords a certain gentleman of great estate and a favourite of his, by name Lorenzo, and sent word to Lucia that she had spent too much of her youth pining for what could not be hers, and must forthwith receive Lorenzo for her husband. But Lucia, being by now a woman and no more a timid girl, returned to His Highness a message that she would look on no other man than Antonio. On this the Duke, greatly incensed, sent and took her, and set her in a convent within the city walls, and made her know that there she should abide till her life's end, or until she should obey his command; and he charged the Abbess to treat her harshly and to break down her pride: and he swore that she should wed Lorenzo; or, if she were obstinate, then she should take the vows of a nun in the convent. Many weeks the Lady Lucia abode in the convent, resisting all that was urged upon her. But at last, finding no help from Antonio, being sore beset and allowed no rest, she broke one day into passionate and pitiful weeping, and bade the Abbess tell His Highness that, since happiness was not for her in this world, she would seek to find it in Heaven, and would take the vows, rendering all her estate into the Duke's hand, that he might have it, and give it to Lorenzo or to whom he would. Which message being told to Duke Valentine, weary of contending with her, and perchance secretly fearing that Antonio would slay Lorenzo as he had slain Robert, he cursed her for an obstinate wench, and bade her take the vows, and set a day for her to take them: but her estate he assumed into his own hand, and made from out of it a gift of great value to Lorenzo. And Lorenzo, they say, was well content thus to be quit of the matter. "For," said he, "while that devil is loose in the hills, no peace would there have been for the lady's husband."

But when it came to the ears of Count Antonio that the Lady Lucia was to take the veil on the morrow of the feast of St. Prisian, his rage and affliction knew no bounds. "If need be," he cried, "I will attack the city with all my men, before I will suffer it."

"Your men would be all killed, and she would take the veil none the less," said Tommasino. For Antonio had but fifty men, and although they were stout fellows and impossible to subdue so long as they stayed in the hills, yet their strength would have been nothing against a fortress and the Duke's array.

"Then," said Antonio, "I will go alone and die alone."

As he spoke, he perceived Martolo coming to him, and, calling him, he asked him what he would. Now Martolo was a devout man and had been much grieved when Antonio had fallen under a sentence of excommunication by reason of a certain quarrel that he had with the Abbot of the Abbey of St. Prisian in the hills, wherein the Count had incurred the condemnation of the Church, refusing, as his way was, to admit any rule save of his own conscience. Yet Martolo abode with Antonio from love of him. And now he bowed and answered, "My lord, in three days it is the feast of St. Prisian, and the sacred bones will then be carried from the shrine in the church of the saint at Rilano to the city." For it was at Rilano that Prisian had suffered, and a rich church had been built on the spot.

"I remember that it is wont to be so, Martolo," answered the Count.

"When I dwelt with my father," said Martolo, "I was accustomed to go forth with all the people of my village and meet the sacred bones, and kneeling, receive the benediction from the Lord Archbishop as he passed, bearing the bones in their golden casket. And the like I would do this year, my lord."

"But are you not excommunicated in company with Count Antonio and me?" asked Tommasino, lightly smiling; for Tommasino also stood condemned.

"I pray not. I was not named in the sentence," said Martolo, signing the cross.

"Go in peace, Martolo; but see that you are not taken by the Duke's men," said Count Antonio.

"But few of them go with the Archbishop, my lord. For who would lay hands on the sacred bones? The guard is small, and I shall easily elude them." So Martolo departed, and told the man they called Bena what had passed; but Bena was a graceless fellow and would not go with him.

Now when Martolo was gone, Count Antonio sat down on a great stone and for a long while he said nothing to Tommasino. But certain words out of those which Martolo had spoken were echoing through his brain, and he could not put them aside; for they came again and again and again; and at last, looking up at Tommasino who stood by him, he said, "Tommasino, who would lay hands on the sacred bones?"

Tommasino looked down into his eyes; then he laid a hand on his shoulder; and Antonio still looked up and repeated, "Who would lay hands on the sacred bones?"

Tommasino's eyes grew round in wonder: he smiled, but his smile was uneasy, and he shifted his feet. "Is it that you think of, Antonio?" he asked in a low voice. "Beside it, it would be a light thing to kill the Duke in his own palace."

Then Antonio cried, striking his fist on the palm of his hand, "Are dead bones more sacred than that living soul on which the Duke lays hands to force it to his will?"

"The people reverence the bones as God Himself," said Tommasino, troubled.

"I also reverence them," said Antonio, and fell again into thought. But presently he rose and took Tommasino's arm, and for a long while they walked to and fro. Then they went and sought out certain chosen men of the band; for the greater part they dared not trust in such a matter, but turned only to them that were boldest and recked least of sacred things. To ten of such Antonio opened his counsel; and by great rewards he prevailed on them to come into the plan, although they were, for all their boldness, very sore afraid lest they, laying hands on the bones, should be smitten as was he who touched the Ark of the Covenant. Therefore Antonio said, "I alone will lay hands on the golden casket; the rest of you shall but hold me harmless while I take it."

"But if the Lord Archbishop will not let it go?"

"The Lord Archbishop," said Tommasino, "will let it go." For Tommasino did not love the Archbishop, because he would not remove the sentence of excommunication which he had laid upon Antonio and Tommasino on the prayer of the Abbot of St. Prisian's.

Now when the feast of St. Prisian was come, the Lord Archbishop, who had ridden from the city on the eve of the feast, and had lodged in the house of the priests that served the church, went with all his train into the church, and, the rest standing afar off and veiling their eyes, took from the wall of the church, near by the High Altar, the golden casket that held the bones of the blessed St. Prisian. And he wrapped the casket in a rich cloth and held it high before him in his two hands. And when the people had worshipped, the Archbishop left the church and entered his chair and passed through the village of Rilano, the priests and attendants going first, and twelve of the Duke's Guard, whom the Duke had sent, following after. Great was the throng of folk, come from all the country round to gaze on the casket and on the procession of the Lord Archbishop; and most devout of them all was Martolo, who rested on his knees from the moment the procession left the church till it was clear of the village. And Martolo was still on his knees when he beheld go by him a party of peasants, all, save one, tall and powerful men, wearing peasants' garb and having their faces overshadowed by large hats. These men also had knelt as the casket passed, but they had risen, and were marching shoulder to shoulder behind the men of the Duke's Guard, a peasant behind every pikeman. Martolo gazed long at them; then he moistened his lips and crossed himself, murmuring, "What does this thing mean? Now God forbid——!" And, breaking off thus, he also rose and went to the house of his father, sore vexed and troubled to know what the thing might mean. But he spoke of it to none, no, not to his father, observing the vow of secrecy in all matters which he had made to Count Antonio.

At the bounds of the village the greater part of the people ceased to follow the procession of the sacred bones, and, having received the Archbishop's blessing, turned back to their own homes, where they feasted and made merry; but the twelve peasants whom Martolo had seen followed the procession when it set forth for the next village, distant three miles on the road to Firmola. Their air manifested great devotion, for they walked with heads bent on their breasts and downcast eyes, and they spoke not once on the way; but each kept close behind a pikeman. When the procession had gone something more than a mile from the village of Rilano, it came where a little stream crosses the highway; and the rains having been heavy for a week before, the stream was swollen and the ford deeper than it was wont to be. Therefore the officer of the Guard, thinking of no danger, bade six of his men lay down their pikes and go lift the Archbishop's chair over the ford, lest the Archbishop should be wetted by the water. And on hearing this order, the tallest among the peasants put his hand up to his hat and twisted the feather of it between his thumb and his forefinger: and the shortest of them whispered, "The sign! The sign!" while every man of them drew a great dagger from under his habit and held it behind his back. Now by this time the priests and attendants had passed the ford; and one-half of the Guard had laid down their pikes and were gone to raise the Archbishop's chair, the remainder standing at their ease, leaning on their pikes and talking to one another. Again the tallest peasant twisted the feather in his hat; and without speech or cry the peasants darted forward. Six of them seized the pikes that lay on the ground; the remaining six sprang like wild-cats on the backs of the pikemen, circling the necks of the pikemen with their arms, pulling them back and coming near to throttling them, so that the pikemen, utterly amazed and taken full at disadvantage, staggered and fell backward, while the peasants got on the top of them and knelt on their breasts and set the great daggers at their hearts. While this passed on the road, the remainder of Antonio's band —for such were the peasants—rushed into the stream and compelled the unarmed pikemen to set down the Archbishop's chair in the midst, so that the water came in at the windows of the chair; and the pikemen, held at bay with their own pikes, sought to draw their poniards, but Antonio cried, "Slay any that draw!" And he came to the chair and opened the door of it, and, using as little force as he might, he laid hands on the casket that held the sacred bones, and wrested it from the feeble hands of the Archbishop. Then he and his men, standing in line, stepped backwards with the pikes levelled in front of them till they came out of the water and on to the dry road again; and one pikeman rushed at Antonio, but Tommasino, sparing to kill him, caught him a buffet on the side of the head with a pike, and he fell like a log in the water, and had been drowned, but that two of his comrades lifted him. Then all twelve of the band being together—for the first six had risen now from off the six pikemen, having forced them, on pain of instant death, to deliver over their pikes to them—Antonio, with the casket in his hands, spoke in a loud voice, "I thank God that no man is dead over this business; but if you resist, you shall die one and all. Go to the city; tell the Duke that I, Antonio of Monte Velluto, have the bones of the blessed St. Prisian, and carry them with me to my hiding-place in the highest parts of the hills. But if he will swear by these bones that I hold, and by his princely word, that he will not suffer the Lady

Lucia to take the vows, nor will constrain her to wed any man, but will restore her to her own house and to her estate, then let him send the Archbishop again, and I will deliver up the sacred bones. But if he will not swear, then, as God lives, to-morrow, at midnight, I will cause a great fire to be kindled on the top of the hills—a fire whose flame you shall see from the walls of the city—and in that fire will I consume the sacred bones, and I will scatter the ashes of them to the four winds. Go and bear the message that I give you to the Duke."

And, having thus said, Antonio, with his men, turned and went back at a run along the road by which they had come; but to the village of Rilano they did not go, but turned aside before they came to it, and, coming to the farm of one who knew Antonio, they bought of him, paying him in good coin of the Duchy, three horses, which Antonio, Tommasino, and Bena mounted; and they three rode hard for the hills, the rest following as quickly as they might; so that by nightfall they were all safely assembled in their hiding-place, and with them the bones of the blessed St. Prisian. But they told not yet to the rest of the band what it was that Antonio carried under his cloak; nor did Martolo, when he returned from Rilano, ask what had befallen, but he crossed himself many times and wore a fearful look.

But Tommasino came to Antonio and said to him, "Why did you not ask also pardon for all of us, and for yourself the hand of Lucia?"

"A great thing, and a thing that troubles me, I have done already," answered Antonio. "Therefore I will ask nothing for myself, and nothing may I ask for you or for my friends. But if I ask nothing save that right and justice be done, it may be that my sin in laying hands on the sacred bones will be the less."

Now after Antonio and his men were gone, the Archbishop's train stayed long by the stream on the road, lamenting and fearing to go forward. Yet at last they went forward, and being come to the next village found all the people awaiting them at the bounds. And when the people saw the disorder of the procession, and that the pikemen had no pikes, they ran forward, eagerly asking what had befallen; and learning of the calamity, they were greatly afraid and cursed Antonio; and many of them accompanied the Archbishop on his way to the city, whence he came towards evening. A great concourse of people awaited his coming there, and the Duke himself sat on a lofty seat in the great square, prepared to receive the sacred bones, and go with them to the Cathedral, where they were to be exposed to the gaze of the people at High Mass. And they set the Archbishop's chair down before the Duke's seat, and the Archbishop came and stood before the Duke, and his priests and the pikemen with him. And the Duke started up from his seat, crying, "What ails you?" and sank back again, and sat waiting to hear what the Archbishop should say.

Then the Archbishop, his robes still damp and greatly disordered, his limbs trembling in anger and in fear, raised his voice; and all the multitude in the square was silent while he declared to His Highness what things Count Antonio had done, and rehearsed the message that he had sent. But when the Archbishop told how Antonio had sworn that as God lived he would scatter the ashes of the sacred bones to the winds, the men caught their breath with a gasp, while the women murmured affrightedly, "Christ save us;" and Duke Valentine dug the nails of his hand, whereon his head rested, into the flesh of his cheek. For all the city held that, according to the words St. Prisian himself had uttered before he suffered, the power and prosperity of the Duchy and the favour of Heaven to it rested on the presence among them and the faithful preservation and veneration of those most holy relics. And the Archbishop, having ended the message, cried, "God pardon my lips that repeat such words," and fell on his knees before Duke Valentine, crying, "Justice on him, my lord, justice!" And many in the throng echoed his cry; but others, and among them a great part of the apprenticed lads who loved Antonio, muttered low one to another, "But the Duke has taken his sweetheart from him," and they looked on the Duke with no favourable eye.

Then Duke Valentine rose from his seat and stood on the topmost step that led to it, and he called sundry of his lords and officers round him, and then he beckoned for silence, and he said, "Before the sun sets to-morrow, the Lady Lucia shall take the vows;" and he, with his train, took their way to the palace, the pikemen clearing a path for them. And now indeed was silence; for all marvelled and were struck dumb that the Duke said naught concerning the bones of St. Prisian, and they searched one another's faces for the meaning of his words. But the Archbishop arose, and, speaking to no man, went to the Cathedral, and knelt before the altar in the chapel of St. Prisian, and there abode on his knees.

Surely never, from that day until this hour, has such a night passed in the city of Firmola. For the Duke sent orders that every man of his Guard should be ready to start at break of day in pursuit of Antonio, and through the hours of the evening they were busied in preparing their provisions and accoutrements. But their looks were heavy and their tongues tied, for they knew, every man of them, that though the Duke might at the end take Antonio, yet he could not come at him before the time that Antonio had said. And this the townsmen knew well also; and they gathered themselves in groups in the great square, saying, "Before the Duke comes at him, the sacred bones will be burnt, and what will then befall the Duchy?" And those who were friendly to Antonio, foremost among them being the apprenticed lads, spread themselves here and there among the people, asking cunningly whether it concerned the people of Firmola more that the blessing of St. Prisian should abide with them, or that a reluctant maiden should be forced to take the veil; and some grew bold to whisper under their breath that the business was a foul one, and that Heaven did not send beauty and love that priests should bury them in convent walls. And the girls of the city, ever most bold by reason of their helplessness, stirred up the young men who courted them, leading them on and saying, "He is a true lover who risks his soul for his love;" or, "I would I had one who would steal the bones of St. Prisian for my sake, but none such have I:" with other stirring and inflaming taunts, recklessly flung from pouting lips and from under eyes that challenged. And all the while Duke Valentine sat alone in his cabinet, listening to the tumult that sounded with muffled din through the walls of the palace.

Now there was in the city a certain furrier named Peter, a turbulent fellow who had been put out of his craft-guild because he would not abide by the laws of the craft, and lived now as he best could, being maintained in large measure by those who listened to his empty and seditious conversation. This man, loving naught that there was worthy of love in Count Antonio, yet loved him because he defied the Duke; and about midnight, having drunk much wine, he came into the square and gathered together the apprentices, saying, "I have a matter to say to you—and to you—and to you," till there were many scores of them round him: then he harangued them, and more came round; and when at last Peter cried, "Give us back the sacred bones!" a thousand voices answered him, "Aye, give us back the bones!" And when the pikemen would have seized him, men, and women also, made a ring round him, so that he could not be taken. And sober men also, of age and substance, hearkened to him, saying, "He is a knave, but he speaks truth now." So that a very great throng assembled, every man having a staff, and many also knives; and to those that had not knives, the women and girls brought them, thrusting them into their hands; nay, sundry priests also were among the people, moaning and wringing their hands, and saying that the favour of St. Prisian would be lost for ever to the city. And the square was thronged, so that a man could not move unless all moved, nor raise his hand to his head save by the favour of his neighbour. Yet presently the whole mass began to move, like a great wave of water, towards the Palace of the Duke, where the pikemen stood in ranks, ready now to go against Antonio. Suddenly arose a cry, "The Archbishop comes!" and the venerable man was seen, led through the crowd by Peter and some more, who brought him and set him in the front ranks of the people; and Peter cried boldly, "Where is the Duke?" But the Captain of the Guard came forward, sword in hand, and bade Peter be still, cursing him for insolence, and shouted that the people should disperse on pain of His Highness's displeasure. "Where is the Duke? Let him come out to us!" cried Peter; and the captain, despising him, struck him lightly with the flat of his sword. But Peter with a cry of rage struck the captain a great blow with his staff, and the captain staggered back, blood flowing from his head. Such was the beginning of the fray; for in an instant the pikemen and the people had joined battle: men cried in anger and women in fright: blood flowed, and sundry on both sides fell and rose no more; and the Archbishop came near to being trodden under foot till his friends and the priests gathered round him; and when he saw that men were being slain, he wept.

Then the lord Lorenzo hastened to the cabinet of the Duke, whom he found pacing up and down, gnawing his finger-nails, and told him of what was done outside.

"I care not," said the Duke. "She shall take the vows! Let the pikemen scatter them."

Lorenzo then besought him, telling him that

all the city was in arms, and that the conflict would be great. But the Duke said still, "She shall take the vows!" Nevertheless he went with Lorenzo, and came forth on to the topmost step of the portico. And when the people saw him they ceased for a moment to assail the pikemen, and cried out, "Give us back the sacred bones!"

"Scatter these fellows!" said the Duke to the Captain of the Guard.

"My lord, they are too many. And if we scatter them now, yet when we have gone against Count Antonio, they may do what they will with the city."

The Duke stood still, pale, and again gnawing his nails; and the pikemen, finding the fight hard, gave back before the people; and the people pressed on.

Then Peter the furrier came forward, and the hottest with him, and mocked the pikemen; and one of the pikemen suddenly thrust Peter through with his pike, and the fellow fell dead; on which a great cry of rage rose from all the people, and they rushed on the pikemen again and slew and were slain; and the fight rolled up the steps even to the very feet of the Duke himself. And at last, able no longer to contend with all the city, he cried, "Hold! I will restore the sacred bones!" But the people would not trust him and one cried, "Bring out the lady here before us and set her free, or we will burn the palace." And the Archbishop came suddenly and threw himself on his knees before the Duke, beseeching him that no more blood might be shed, but that the Lady Lucia should be set free. And the Duke, now greatly afraid, sent hastily the Lieutenant of the Guard and ten men, who came to the convent where Lucia was, and, brooking no delay, carried her with them in her bedgown, and brought and set her beside the Duke in the portico of the palace. Then the Duke raised his hand to heaven, and before all the people he said, "Behold, she is free! Let her go to her own house, and her estate shall be hers again. And by my princely word and these same holy bones, I swear that she shall not take the vows, neither will I constrain her to wed any man." And when he had said this, he turned sharply round on his heel, and, looking neither to the right nor to the left, went through the great hall to his cabinet and shut the door. For his heart was very sore that he must yield to Antonio's demand, and for himself he had rather a thousand times that the bones of St. Prisian had been burnt.

Now when the Duke was gone, the people brought the Lady Lucia to her own house, driving out the steward whom the Duke had set there, and, this done, they came to the Archbishop, and would not suffer him to rest or to delay one hour before he set forth to carry the Duke's promise to Antonio. This the Archbishop was ready to do, for all that he was weary. But first he sent Lorenzo to ask the Duke's pleasure; and Lorenzo, coming to the Duke, prayed him to send two hundred pikes with the Archbishop. "For," said he, "your Highness has sworn nothing concerning what shall befall Antonio; and so soon as he has delivered up the bones, I will set on him and bring him alive or dead to your Highness."

But the Duke would not hearken. "The

fellow's name is like stale lees of wine in my mouth," said he. "Ten of my pikemen lie dead in the square, and more of the citizens. I will lose no more men over it."

"Yet how great a thing if we could take him!"

"I will take him at my own time and in my own way," said the Duke. "In God's name, leave me now."

Lorenzo therefore got from the Duke leave for but ten men to go with the Archbishop, and to go himself if he would. And thus they set out, exhorted by the people, who followed them beyond the bounds of the city, to make all speed. And when they were gone, the people came back and took up the bodies of the dead; while the pikemen also took up the bodies of such of their comrades as were slain.

Yet had Duke Valentine known what passed on the hills while the city was in tumult, it may not be doubted, for all his vexation, that he would have sent the two hundred whom Lorenzo asked: never had he a fairer chance to take Antonio. For when the Count and those who had been with him to Rilano were asleep, Antonio's head resting on the golden casket, a shepherd came to the rest of the band and told them what had been done and how all the country was in an uproar. Then a debate arose amongst the band, for, though they were lawless men, yet they feared God, and thought with great dread on what Antonio had sworn; so that presently they came altogether, and aroused Antonio, and said to him, "My lord, you have done much for us, and it may be that we have done somewhat for you. But we will not suffer the sacred bones to be burnt and scattered to the winds."

"Except the Duke yields, I have sworn it, as God lives," answered Antonio.

"We care not. It shall not be, no, not though you and we die," said they.

"It is well; I hear," said Antonio, bowing his head.

"In an hour," said they, "we will take the bones, if you will not yourself, my lord, send them back."

"Again I hear," said Antonio, bowing his head; and the band went back to the fire round which they had been sitting, all save Martolo, who came and put his hand in Antonio's hand.

"How now, Martolo?" asked Antonio.

"What you will, I will, my lord," said Martolo. For though he trembled when he thought of the bones of St. Prisian, yet he clung always to Antonio. As for Bena and the others of the ten who had gone to Rilano, they would now have burnt not the bones only, but the blessed saint himself, had Antonio bidden them. Hard men, in truth, were they, and the more reckless now, because no harm had come to them from the seizing of the bones; moreover Antonio had given them good wine for supper, and they drank well.

Now the rest of the band being gone back to their fire and the night being very dark, in great silence and caution Antonio, Tommasino, Martolo, Bena, and their fellows—being thirteen in all—rose from their places, and taking naught with them but their swords (save that Antonio carried the golden casket), they stole forth from the camp, and set their faces to climb yet higher into the heights of the hills. None spoke; one following another, they climbed the steep path that led up the mountain side; and when they had been going for the space of an hour, they heard a shout from far below them.

"Our flight is known," said Tommasino.

"Shall we stand and meet them, my lord?" asked Bena.

"Nay, not yet," said Antonio; and the thirteen went forward again at the best speed they could.

Now they were in a deep gorge between lofty cliffs; and the gorge still tended upwards; and at length they came to the place which is now named "Antonio's Neck." There the rocks came nigh to meeting and utterly barring the path; yet there is a way that one man, or at most two, may pass through at one time. Along this narrow tongue they passed, and, coming to the other side, found a level space on the edge of a great precipice, and Antonio pointing over the precipice, they saw in the light of the day, which now was dawning, the towers and spires of Firmola very far away in the plain below.

"It is a better place for the fire than the

other," said Antonio; and Bena laughed, while Martolo shivered.

"Yet we risk being hindered by these fellows behind," said Tommasino.

"Nay, I think not," said Antonio.

Then he charged Tommasino and all of them to busy themselves in collecting such dry sticks and brushwood as they could; and there was abundance near, for the fir-trees grew even so high. And one of the men also went and set a snare, and presently caught a wild goat, so that they had meat. But Antonio took Bena and set him on one side of the way where the neck opened out into the level space; and he stood on the other side of the way himself. And when they stretched out their arms, the point of Bena's sword reached the hilt of Antonio's. And Antonio smiled, saying to Bena, "He had need to be a thin man, Bena, that passes between you and me."

And Bena nodded his head at Count Antonio, answering, "Indeed this is as strait as the way to heaven, my lord, and leads, as it seems to me, in much the same direction."

Thus Antonio and Bena waited in the shelter of the rocks at the opening of the neck, while the rest built up a great pile of wood. Then, having roasted the meat, they made their breakfast, Martolo carrying portions to Antonio and to Bena. And, their pursuers not knowing the path so well and therefore moving less quickly, it was but three hours short of noon when they heard the voices of men from the other side of the neck. And Antonio cried straightway, "Come not through at your peril! Yet one may come and speak with me."

Then a great fellow, whose name is variously given, though most of those whom I have questioned call him Sancho, came through the neck, and, reaching the end of it, found the crossed swords of Antonio and Bena like a fence against his breast. And he saw also the great pile of wood, and resting now on the top of it the golden casket that held the sacred bones. And he said to Antonio, "My lord, we love you; but sooner than that the bones should be burnt, we will kill you and all that are with you."

But Antonio answered, "I also love you,

Sancho; yet you and all your company shall die sooner than my oath shall be broken."

"Your soul shall answer for it, my lord," said Sancho.

"You speak truly," answered Antonio.

Then Sancho went back through the neck and took counsel with his fellows; and they made him their chief, and promised to be obedient to all that he ordered. And he said, "Let two run at their highest speed through the neck: it may be they will die, but the bones must be saved. And after them, two more, and again two. And I will be of the first two."

But they would not suffer him to be of the first two, although he prevailed that he should be of the last two. And the six, being chosen, drew their swords and with a cry rushed into the neck. Antonio, hearing their feet, said to Bena, "A quick blow is as good as a slow, Bena." And even as he spoke the first two came to the opening of the neck. But Antonio and Bena struck at them before they came out of the narrowest part or could wield their swords freely; and the second two coming on, Bena struck at one and wounded him in the breast, and he wounded Bena in the face over the right eye, and then Bena slew him; while Antonio slew his man at his first stroke. And the fifth man and Sancho, the sixth, coming on, Antonio cried loudly, "Are you mad, are you mad? We could hold the neck against a hundred."

But they would not stop, and Antonio slew the fifth, and Bena was in the act to strike at Sancho, but Antonio suddenly dashed Sancho's sword from his hand, and caught him a mighty buffet, so that he fell sprawling on the bodies of the five that were dead.

"Go back, fool, go back!" cried Antonio.

And Sancho, answering nothing, gathered himself up and went back; for he perceived now that not with the loss of half of his men would he get by Antonio and Bena; and beyond them stood Tommasino with ten whom he knew to be of the stoutest of the band.

"It is a sore day's work, Bena," cried Antonio, looking at the dead bodies.

"If a man be too great a fool to keep himself alive, my lord, he must die," answered Bena; and he pushed the bodies a little further back into the neck with his foot.

Then Sancho's company took counsel again; for, much as they reverenced the sacred bones, there was none of them eager to enter the neck. Thus they were at a loss, till the shepherd who had come along with them spoke to Sancho, saying, "At the cost of a long journey you may come at him; for there is a way round that I can lead you by. But you will not traverse it in less than twelve or thirteen hours, taking necessary rest by the way."

But Sancho, counting the time, cried, "It will serve! For although a thousand came against him, yet the Count will not burn the bones before the time of his oath."

Therefore he left fifteen men to hold the neck, in case Antonio should offer to return back through it, and with the rest he followed the shepherd in great stealth and quiet; by reason of which, and of the rock between them, Antonio knew not what was done, but thought that the whole company lay still on the other side of the neck.

Thus the day wore to evening as the Archbishop with the Lord Lorenzo and the guards came to the spur of the hills; and here they found a man waiting, who cried to them, "Do you bring the Duke's promise to the Count Antonio?"

"Yes, we bring it," said they.

"I am charged," said he, "to lead the Archbishop and one other after the Count." But since the Archbishop could not climb the hills, being old and weary, Lorenzo constrained the man to take with him four of the Guards besides; and the four bore the Archbishop along. Thus they were led through the secret tracks in the hills, and these Lorenzo tried to engrave on his memory, that he might come again. But the way was long and devious, and it was hard to mark it. Thus going, they came to the huts, and passing the huts, still climbed wearily till they arrived near to the neck. It was then night, and, as they guessed, hard on the time when Antonio had sworn to burn the sacred bones; therefore they pressed on more and more, and came at last to the entrance of the neck. Here they found the fifteen, and Lorenzo, running up, cried aloud, "We bring the promise, we bring the promise!"

But scarcely had he spoken these words, when a sudden great shout came from the other side of the neck; and Lorenzo, drawing his sword, rushed into the neck, the fifteen following, yet leaving a space between him and them, lest they should see him fall, pierced by Antonio and Bena. And Lorenzo stumbled and fell over the five dead bodies which lay in the way of the neck. Uttering a cry, "What are these?" he scrambled again to his feet, and passed unhurt through the mouth of the neck, and the fifteen followed after him, while the Guards supported the Archbishop in their hands, his chair being too wide to pass through the neck. And when thus they all came through, wild and strange was the sight they saw. For it chanced that at the same time Sancho's company had completed their circuit, and had burst from behind upon Antonio and the twelve. And when the twelve saw them, they retreated to the great pile and made a ring round it, and stood there ready to die rather than allow Sancho's men to reach the pile. It was then midnight and the time of Count Antonio's oath. Count Antonio stood on the top of the great pile; at his feet lay the golden casket containing the sacred bones, and in his hand was a torch. And he cried aloud, "Hold them, while I fire the pile!" and he leapt down and came to the side of the pile and laid his torch to the pile. And in an instant the flames shot up, for the pile was dry.

Now when Sancho's men saw the pile alight, with shouts of horror and of terror they charged at the top of their speed against the twelve who guarded the pile. And Lorenzo and his men also rushed; but the cries of Sancho's company, together with the answering defiance of the twelve, drowned the cries of Lorenzo; and Antonio and the twelve knew not that Lorenzo was come. And the flames of the pile grew, and the highest tongue of flame licked the side of the golden casket. But Antonio's voice rose above all, as he stood, aye, almost within the ambit of the fire, and cried, "Hold them a moment, Tommasino—a moment, Bena—and the thing is done!" Then Lorenzo tore his casque from his head and flung down his sword, and rushed unarmed between Antonio's men and Sancho's men, shouting louder than he had thought ever to shout, "The promise! the promise!" And at the same moment (so it is told, I but tell it as it is told) there came from heaven a great flash of lightning, which, aiding the glare of the flames, fully revealed the features of Lorenzo. Back fell Sancho's men, and Antonio's arrested their swords. And then they all cried as men cry in great joy, "The promise! the promise!" And for a moment all stood still where they were. But the flames leapt higher; and, as Antonio had said, they were seen by the great throng that gazed from the city walls; and they were seen by Duke Valentine as he watched from the wall of his garden by the river; and he went pale, gnawing his nails.

Then the Count Antonio sprang on the burning pile, though it seemed that no man could pass alive through it. Yet God was with him, and he gained the top of it, and, stooping, seized the golden casket and flung it down, clear of the pile, even at the Lord Lorenzo's feet; and when Lorenzo sought to lift it, the heat of it blistered his hands, and he cried out with pain. But Count Antonio, choked by the smoke, his hair and his eyebrows scorched by the fire, staggered half-way down the pile and there sank on his knees. And there he had died, but that Tommasino, Bena, and Sancho, each eager to outstrip the other, rushed in and drew him forth, and fetched water and gave it to him, so that he breathed again and lived. But the flames leapt higher and higher; and they said on the city walls, "God help us! God help us! The sacred bones are burnt!" And women, aye, and men too, fell to weeping, and there was great sorrow, fear, and desolation. And the Duke gnawed his nails even to the quick, and spat the blood from his mouth, cursing Antonio.

But Lorenzo, having perceived that the greater number was against Antonio, cried out to Sancho's men, "Seize him and bring him here!" For the Duke's promise carried no safety to Antonio.

But Sancho answered him, "Now that the sacred bones are safe, we have no quarrel with my lord Antonio;" and he and his men went and laid down their swords by the feet of Antonio, where he lay on the ground, his head on Tommasino's lap. So that the whole band were now round Antonio, and Lorenzo had but four with him.

"He asks war!" growled Bena to Tommasino. "Shall he not have war, my lord?"

And Tommasino laughed, answering, "Here is a drunkard of blood!"

But Count Antonio, raising himself, said, "Is the Archbishop here?"

Then Lorenzo went and brought the Archbishop, who, coming, stood before Antonio, and rehearsed to him the oath that Duke Valentine had taken, and told him how the Lady Lucia was already free and in her own house, and made him aware also of the great tumult that had happened in the city. And Antonio listened to his tale in silence.

Then the Archbishop raised a hand towards heaven and spoke in a solemn and sad voice,

"Behold, there are ten of the Duke's Guard dead in the city, and there are twelve of the townsmen dead; and here, in the opening of the neck, there lie dead five men of those who followed you, my lord. Twenty-and-seven men are there that have died over this business. I pray more have not died in the city since I set forth. And for what has this been done, my lord? And more than the death of all these is there. For these sacred bones have been foully and irreligiously stolen and carried away, used with vile irreverence and brought into imminent hazard of utter destruction: and had they been destroyed and their ashes scattered to the four winds, according to your blasphemous oath, I know not what would have befallen the country where such an act was done. And for what has this been done, my lord? It has been done that a proud and violent man may have his will, and that his passion may be satisfied. Heavy indeed is the burden on your soul my lord; yes, on your soul is the weight of sacrilege and of much blood."

The Archbishop ceased, and his hand dropped

to his side. The flames on the pile were burning low, and a stillness fell on all the company. But at last Count Antonio rose to his feet and stood with his elbow on Tommasino's shoulder, leaning on Tommasino. His face was weary and sad, and he was very pale, save where in one spot the flame had scorched his cheek to an angry red. And looking round on the Archbishop, and on the Lord Lorenzo, and on them all, he answered sadly, "In truth, my Lord Archbishop, my burden is heavy. For I am an outlaw, and excommunicated. Twenty-and-seven men have died through my act, and I have used the sacred bones foully, and brought them into imminent peril of total destruction, according to my oath. All this is true, my lord. And yet I know not. For Almighty God, whom all we, whether honest men or knaves, men of law or lawless, humbly worship—Almighty God has His own scales, my lord. And I know not which thing be in those scales the heavier; that twenty-and-seven men should die, and that the bones of the blessed St. Prisian should be brought in peril, aye, or should be utterly destroyed; or again that one weak girl, who has no protection save in the justice and pity of men, should be denied justice and bereft of pity, and that no man should hearken to her weeping. Say, my lord—for it is yours to teach and mine to learn—which of these things should God count the greater sin? And for myself I have asked nothing; and for my friends here, whom I love—yes, even those I have killed for my oath's sake, I loved—I have dared to ask nothing. But I asked only that justice should be done and mercy regarded. Where, my lord, is the greater sin?"

But the Archbishop answered not a word to Count Antonio; but he and the Lord Lorenzo came and lifted the golden casket, and, no man of Antonio's company seeking to hinder them, they went back with it to the city and showed it to the people; and after that the people had rejoiced greatly that the sacred bones, which they had thought to be destroyed, were safe, the Archbishop carried the golden casket back to the shrine in the village of Rilano, where it rests till this day. But Count Antonio buried the five men of his band whom he and Bena had slain, and with the rest he abode still in the hills, while the Lady Lucia dwelt in her own house in the city; and the Duke, honouring the oath which he had sworn before all the people, did not seek to constrain her to wed any man, and restored to her the estate that he had taken from her. Yet the Duke hated Count Antonio the more for what he had done, and sought the more eagerly how he might take him and put him to death.

CHAPTER VI.

COUNT ANTONIO AND THE HERMIT OF THE VAULT.

AMONG the stories concerning the Count Antonio which were told to me in answer to my questioning (whereof I have rejected many as being no better than idle tales), there was one that met me often and yet seemed strange and impossible to believe; for it was said that he had during the time of his outlawry once spent several days in the vault of the Peschetti, and there suffered things that pass human understanding.

This vault lies near to the church of St. John the Theologian, in the suburb of Baratesta, on the banks of the river; and the Peschetti had a palace hard by, and were a family of high nobility, and allied by blood to the house of Monte

Velluto. But I could find no warrant for the story of Antonio's sojourn in the vault, and although many insisted that the tale was true, yet they could not tell how nor why the Count came to be in the vault; until at length I chanced on an aged woman who had heard the truth of the matter from her grandmother, and she made me acquainted with the story, pouring on me a flood of garrulous gossip, from which I have chosen as much as concerns the purpose. And here I set it down; for I believe it to be true, and I would omit nothing that touches the Count, so I can be sure that what I write is based on truth.

When Count Antonio had dwelt in the hills for the space of three years and nine months, it chanced that Cesare, last of the Peschetti, died; and he made a will on his death-bed whereby he bequeathed to Count Antonio his lands and also a store of money, and many ornaments of gold, and jewels; for Antonio's mother had been of the house of the Peschetti, and Cesare loved Antonio, although he had not dared to give him countenance for fear of the

Duke's anger; yet, knowing himself to be dying, he bequeathed everything to him, for the Duke's wrath could not hurt a dead man. And so soon as he was dead, his steward Giuseppe sent secretly and in haste to Antonio, saying, "My lord, you cannot take the lands or the house; but, if you will be wise, come quickly and take the money and the jewels; for I hear that His Highness the Duke, declaring that an outlaw has no right and can inherit nothing, will send and seize the treasure." Now Antonio, though grieved at the death of Cesare, was glad to hear of the treasure; for he was often hard put to it to maintain his company and those who depended on him for bread. So he pondered anxiously how he might reach the palace of the Peschetti and lay hands on the treasure and return safely; for at this time Duke Valentine had posted above a hundred of his Guard in the plain, and this troop watched all the approaches to the hills, so that the band could not ride forth in a body unless it were prepared to do battle with the guards. Nor did Antonio desire to weaken the band, lest the guards, learning that the bravest were away, should venture an attack. Therefore he would not take Tommasino or Bena or any of the stoutest with him; but he took four young men who had come to him from Firmola, having fallen into the Duke's displeasure through brawling with his guards. These he mounted on good horses, and, having made a circuit to avoid the encampment in the plain, he came to Cesare's house on the day before that appointed for the funeral. Giuseppe came to meet him, and led him where the dead man lay, and, after the Count had gazed on his face and kissed his forehead, they two went to the treasury, and Giuseppe delivered the treasure to Antonio; and Antonio made him a present of value and confirmed him in his stewardship, although it was not likely that the Duke would suffer him to exercise any power, inasmuch as His Highness had declared his intention of forfeiting the estate into his own hand.

Now it chanced that one of the young men, being regaled with wine, drank very freely, and began to talk loud and boastfully of his master's achievements as the servants sat under the trees in front of the house; and there was with them a certain tailor, a lame man, who had furnished mourning garments for the funeral. The tailor, learning that Antonio was come, said nothing, and seemed not to hear nor understand the drunken youth's talk; but at an early moment he took his departure and straightway hobbled as fast as his lame leg would let him to the Syndic of Baratesta, a very busy and ambitious fellow, who longed greatly to win the Duke's favour. And the tailor set the price of five pieces of gold and the ordering of a new gown on the news he brought; and the Syndic having agreed, the tailor cried, "Antonio of Monte Velluto is at the house of the Peschetti, and his band is not with him. If you hasten, you may catch him." At this the Syndic exulted very greatly; for the Duke's Commissaries would not arrive to assume possession of the house in his name till the morrow, by which time Antonio would be gone; and the Syndic rubbed his hands, saying, "If I can take him my glory will be great, and the gratitude of His Highness also." And he gathered together all his constables, and hard upon twenty discharged soldiers who dwelt in the town, and the fifteen men of the Duke's who were stationed at Baratesta to gather His Highness's dues; and thus, with a force of about fifty men, he set out in great haste for the house of the Peschetti, and was almost come there, before a little boy ran to Giuseppe crying that the Syndic and all the constables and many besides were coming to the house. And Giuseppe, who had but three menservants of an age to fight, the other five being old (for Cesare had loved to keep those who served him well, even when their power grew less than their will), and moreover perceived that Antonio's four were young and untried, wrung his hands and hastened to the Count with the news, saying, "Yet weak as we are, we can die for you, my lord."

"Heaven forbid!" said Antonio, looking out of the window. "Are they all townsmen that come with this Syndic?"

"Alas, no, my lord. There are certain of the Duke's men, and I see among the rest men who have spent their days under arms, either in His Highness's service or in Free Companies."

"Then," said Antonio, smiling, "unless I am to share Cesare's funeral, I had best be gone. For I have seen too much fighting to be ashamed to run away from it."

"But, my lord, they are at the gates."

"And is there no other gate?"

"None, my lord, save the little gate in the wall there; and see, the Syndic has posted ten men there."

"And he will search the house?"

"I fear that he will, my lord. For he must have tidings of your coming."

"Then where is my horse?" said Count Antonio; and Giuseppe showed him where the horse stood in the shadow of the portico. "Do not let the Syndic know," added Antonio, "that the young men are of my company, and send them away in safety."

"But what do you, my lord?" cried Giuseppe.

"What I have done before, Giuseppe. I ride for life," answered the Count.

Then the Count, delaying no more, ran lightly down the stairs, leapt on his horse, and, drawing his sword, rode forth from the portico; and he

was among the Syndic's company before they
thought to see him; and he struck right and left
with his sword; and they fell back before him
in fear, yet striking at him as they shrank away;
and he had come clean off, but for one grizzly-
haired fellow who had served much in Free
Companies and learnt cunning; for he stooped
low, avoiding the sweep of Antonio's sword, and
stabbed the horse in its belly, and stood wiping
his knife and saying, "My legs are old. I have
done my part. Do yours; the horse will not go
far." In truth the horse was wounded to death,
and its bowels protruded from the wound; and
Antonio felt it falter and stumble. Yet the gallant beast carried him for half a mile, and then
he sprang off, fearing it would fall under him
as he sat and he be crushed by it; and he drew
his sword across its throat that it might not
linger in pain, and then ran on foot, hearing the
cries of the Syndic's company as it pressed on
behind him. And thus, running, he came to the
church of St. John and to the vault of the
Peschetti by it; two men were at work preparing
for Cesare's funeral, and the door of the vault

was open. Antonio hurled one man to the right and the other to the left, and rushed into the vault; for his breath failed, and there was no chance for his life were he overtaken in the open; and before the men regained their feet, he pulled the door of the vault close and sank on his knee inside, panting, and holding his sword in readiness to slay any who entered. Then the Syndic and his company came and called on him to surrender. And Antonio cried, "Come and take me." Then the Syndic bade the workmen pull open the door; but Antonio held it with one hand against them both. Yet at last they drew it a little open; and Antonio lunged with his sword through the aperture and wounded the Syndic in the leg, so that he stumbled backwards with an oath. And after that none was willing to enter first, until the grizzly-haired fellow came up; but he, seeing the aperture, rushed at it sword in hand, fearing no man, not even Count Antonio. But he could not touch Antonio, and he also fell back with a sore gash in his cheek; and Antonio laughed, saying, "Shall I surrender, Syndic?"

Now the Syndic was very urgent in his desire to take Antonio, but his men shook their heads, and he himself could not stand because of the sword-thrust in his leg; and, instead of fighting, his company began to tell of the wonderful deeds Antonio had done, and they grew no bolder by this; and the grizzly-haired fellow mocked them, saying that he would go again at the aperture if two more would attempt it with him; but none offered. And the Syndic raged and rebuked them, but he could not hurt them, being unable to stand on his feet; so that one said boldly, "Why should we die? The Duke's Commissaries will be here to-morrow with a company of the Guard. Let the Count stay in the vault till then. He is in safe keeping; and when he sees the Guard he will surrender. It is likely enough that a great lord like the Count would rather die than give up his sword to the Syndic." Whereat the Syndic was very ill pleased, but all the rest mighty well pleased; and, having heard this counsel, they could by no means be persuaded to attack afresh, but they let Antonio draw the door close again, being in truth glad to see the last of his sword. Therefore the Syndic, having no choice, set twenty to guard the entrance of the vault and prepared to depart. But he cried to Antonio, again bidding him to surrender, for the Guard would come to-morrow, and then at least he could not hope to resist.

"Aye, but to-morrow is to-morrow, Master Syndic," laughed Antonio. "Go, get your leg dressed, and leave to-morrow till it dawn."

So the Syndic went home and the rest with him, leaving the twenty on guard. And to this day, if a man hath more love for fighting than skill in it, folk call him a Syndic of Baratesta.

Count Antonio, being thus left in the vault, and perceiving that he would not be further molested that day, looked round; and though no daylight reached the vault, he could see, for the workmen had set a lamp there and it still burnt. Around him were the coffins of all the Peschetti who had died in five hundred years; and the air was heavy and stifling. Antonio took the lamp and walked round the vault, which was of circular form; and he perceived one coffin standing upright against the wall of the vault, as though there had been no room for it on the shelves. Then he sat down again, and, being weary, leant his head against the wall and soon slept; for a man whose conscience is easy and whose head has sense in it may sleep as well in a vault as in a bedchamber. Yet the air of the vault oppressed him, and he slept but lightly and uneasily. And, if a proof be needed how legends gather round the Count's name, I have heard many wonderful stories of what happened to him in the vault; how he held converse with dead Peschetti, how they told him things which it is not given to men to know, and how a certain beautiful lady, who had been dead two hundred years, having been slain by her lover in a jealous rage, came forth from the coffin, with her hair all dishevelled and a great wound yet bleeding in her bosom, and sang a low sweet wild love-song to him as he lay, and would not leave him though he bade her soul rest in the name of Christ and the Saints. But that any of these things happened I do not believe.

It was late when the Count awoke, and the lamp had burnt out, so that the vault was utterly dark. And as the Count roused himself, a sound strange in the place fell on his ear; for a man talked, and his talk was not such as one uses who speaks aloud his own musings to himself when he is alone (a trick men come by who live solitary), but he seemed to question others and to answer them, saying, "Aye," and "No," and "Alas, sweet friend!" and so forth, all in a low even voice; and now and again he would sigh, and once he laughed bitterly. Then the Count raised his voice, "Who is there?" And the other voice answered, "Which of you speaks? The tones are not known to me. Yet I know all the Peschetti who are here." And Antonio answered, "I am not of the Peschetti save by my mother; my name is Antonio of Monte Velluto." On this a cry came from the darkness, as of a man greatly troubled and alarmed; and after that there was silence for a space. And Antonio said, "There is naught to fear; I seek to save myself, not to hurt another. But how do you, a living man, come to be in this vault, and with whom do you speak?" Then came the sound of steel striking on a flint, and presently a spark, and a torch was lighted; and Antonio beheld before him, in the glow of the torch, the figure of a man who crouched on the floor of the vault over against him; his hair was long and tangled, his beard grew to his waist, and he was naked save for a cloth about his loins; and his eyes gleamed dark and wild as he gazed on Antonio in seeming fright and bewilderment. Then the Count, knowing that a man collects his thoughts while another speaks, told the man who he was and how he came there, and (because the man's eyes still wondered) how that he was an outlaw these three years and more because he would not bow to the Duke's will: and when he had told all, he ceased. Then the man came crawling closer to him, and, holding the torch to his face, scanned his face, saying, "Surely he is alive!" And again he was silent, but after a while he spoke.

"For twenty-and-three years," he said, "I have dwelt here among the dead; and to the dead I talk, and they are my friends and companions. For I hear their voices, and they come out of their coffins and greet me; yet now they are silent and still because you are here."

"But how can you live here?" cried Antonio. "For you must starve for lack of food, and come near to suffocation in the air of this vault."

The man set his hand to his brow and frowned, and said sadly, "Indeed I have forgotten much, yet I remember a certain night when the Devil came into me, and in black fury and jealousy I laid wait by the door of the room where my wife was; and we had been wedded but a few months. There was a man who was my friend, and he came to my wife secretly, seeking to warn her that I was suspected of treason to the Prince: yes, in all things he was my friend; for when I stabbed him as he came to the door, and, rushing in, stabbed her also, she did not die till she had told me all; and then she smiled sweetly at me, saying, "Our friend will forgive, dear husband, for you did not know; and I forgive the blow your love dealt me: kiss me and let me die here in your arms." And I kissed her, and she died. Then I laid her on her bed, and I went forth from my home; and I wandered many days. Then I sought to kill myself, but I could not, for a voice seemed to say, 'What penitence is there in death? Lo, it is sweet, Paolo!' So I did not kill myself; but I took an oath to live apart from men till God should in His mercy send me death. And coming in my wanderings to the river that runs by Baratesta, I found a little hollow in the bank of the river, and I lay down there; and none pursued me, for the Duke of Firmola cared not for a crime done in Mantivoglia. And for a year I dwelt in my little cave: then it was noised about that I dwelt there, and fools began to call me, who was the vilest sinner born, a holy hermit, and they came to me to ask prayers. So I begged from one a pick, and I worked on the face of the rock, and made a passage through it. And I swore to look no more on the light of the sun, but abode in the recesses that I had hollowed out. And I go no more to the mouth of the cave, save once a day at nightfall, when I drink of the water of the river and take the broken meats they leave for me."

"But here—how came you here?" cried Antonio.

"I broke through one day by chance, as I worked on the rock; and, seeing the vault, I made a passage with much labour; and having done this, I hid it with a coffin; and now I dwell here with the dead, expecting the time when in God's mercy I also shall be allowed to die. But to-day I fled back through the passage, for men came and opened the vault and let in the sunshine, which I might not see. Pray for me, sir; I have need of prayers."

"Now God comfort you," said Count Antonio softly. "Of a truth, sir, a man who knows his sin and grieves for it in his heart hath in God's eyes no longer any sin. So is it sweetly taught in the most Holy Scriptures. Therefore take comfort; for your friend will forgive even as the gentle lady who loved you forgave; and Christ has no less forgiveness than they."

"I know not," said the hermit, groaning heavily. "I question the dead who lie here concerning these things, but they may not tell me."

"Indeed, poor man, they can tell nothing," said Antonio gently; for he perceived that the man was subject to a madness and deluded by fancied visions and voices.

"Yet I love to talk to them of the time when I also shall be dead."

"God comfort you," said Count Antonio again.

Now while Antonio and the hermit talked, one of those who guarded the vault chanced to lay his ear against the door, listening whether Antonio moved, and he heard, to his great dread and consternation, the voice of another who talked with Antonio: most of what was said he did not hear, but he heard Antonio say, "God comfort you," and the hermit answer something and groan heavily. And the legs of the listener shook under him, and he cried to his comrades that the dead talked with Antonio, he himself being from fright more dead than alive. Then all came and listened; and still the voice of another talked with Antonio; so that the guards were struck with terror and looked in one another's faces, saying, "The dead speak! The Count speaks with the dead! Christ and the Blessed Mother of Christ and the Saints protect us!" And they looked neither to right nor left, but sat quaking on the ground about the door of the vault; and presently one ran and told the Syndic, and he caused himself to be carried thither in his chair; and he also heard, and was very greatly afraid, saying, "This Antonio of Monte Velluto is a fearful man." And the report spread throughout Baratesta that Count Antonio talked with the dead in the vault of the Peschetti; whence came, I doubt not, the foolish tales of which I have made mention. A seed is enough: men's tongues water it and it grows to a great plant. Nor did any man think that it was the hermit who talked; for although they knew of his cave, they did not know nor imagine of the passage he had made, and his voice was utterly strange, seeing that he had spoken no word to any living man for twenty years, till he spoke with the Count that night. Therefore the whole of Baratesta was in great fear; and they came to a certain learned priest, who was priest of the church of St. John, and told him. And he arose and came in great haste, and offered prayers outside the vault, and bade the unquiet spirits rest; but he did not offer to enter, nor did any one of them; but they all said, "We had determined even before to await the Duke's Guard, and that is still the wiser thing."

For a great while the hermit could not understand what Antonio wanted of him; for his thoughts were on his own state and with the dead; but at length having understood that Antonio would be guided through the passage and brought to the mouth of the cave, in the hope of finding means to escape before the Duke's Commissaries came with the Guard, he murmured wonderingly, "Do you then desire to live?" and rose, and led Antonio where the coffin stood upright against the wall as Antonio had seen it; but it was now moved a little to one side, and there was a narrow opening, through which the Count had much ado to pass; and in his struggles he upset the coffin, and it fell with a great crash; whereat all who were outside the vault fled suddenly to a distance of a hundred yards or more in panic, expecting now to see the door of the vault open and the dead walk forth: nor could they be persuaded to come nearer again. But Antonio, with a great effort, made his way through the opening, and followed the hermit along a narrow rough-hewn way, Antonio's shoulders grazing the rock on either side as he went; and having pursued this way for fifteen or twenty paces, they turned to the right sharply, and went on another ten paces, and, having passed through another narrow opening, were in the cave; and the river glistened before their eyes, for it was now dawn. And the hermit, perceiving that it was dawn, and fearing to see the sun, turned to flee back to the vault; but Antonio, being full of pity for him, detained him, and besought him to abandon his manner of life, assuring him that certainly by now his sin was purged: and when the hermit would not listen, Antonio followed him back to the opening that led into the vault, and, forgetting his own peril, reasoned with him for the space of an hour or more, but could not prevail. So at last he bade him farewell very sorrowfully, telling him that God had made him that day the instrument of saving a man's life, which should be to him a sign of favour and forgiveness; but the hermit shook his head and passed into the vault, and Antonio heard him again talking to the dead Peschetti, and answering questions that his own disordered brain invented.

Thus it was full morning when Antonio came again to the little cave by the river, and bethought him what he should do for his own safety. And suddenly, looking across the river, he beheld a gentleman whom he knew, one Lepardo, a Commissary of the Duke's, and with him thirty of the Duke's Guard; and they were riding very fast; for, having started at midnight to avoid the heat of the sun (it being high summer), so soon as they reached the outskirts of Baratesta, they had heard that Antonio was in the vault, and were now pressing on to cross the bridge and come upon him. And Antonio knew that Lepardo was a man of courage and hardihood, and would be prevented by nothing from entering the vault. But on a sudden Lepardo checked his horse, uttering a loud cry; for to his great amazement he had seen Antonio as Antonio looked forth from the cave, and he could not tell how he came to be there: and Antonio at once withdrew himself into the shadow of the cave. Now the banks of the stream on the side on which Lepardo rode were high and precipitous, and, although it was summer, yet the stream was too deep for him to wade, and flowed quickly; yet at Lepardo's bidding, six of his stoutest men prepared to leap down the bank and go in search of Antonio; and Antonio, discerning that they would do this, and blaming himself for his rashness in looking out so incautiously, was greatly at a loss what to do; for now he was hemmed in on either side; and he saw nothing but· to sell his life dearly and do some deed that should ornament his death. So he retreated again along the passage and passed through the opening into the vault; and he summoned the hermit to aid him, and between them they set not one only, but a dozen of the coffins of the Peschetti against the opening, laying them lengthwise and piling one on the top of the other hoping that Lepardo's men would not discover the opening, or would at least be delayed some time before they could thrust away the coffins and come through. Then Antonio took his place by the gate of the vault again, sword in hand, saying grimly to the hermit, "If you seek Death, sir, he will be hereabouts before long."

But the Count Antonio was not a man whom his friends would abandon to death unaided; and while the Syndic was watching Antonio, the four young men who were with the Count made their escape from Cesare's house; and, having separated from one another, rode by four different ways towards the hills, using much wariness. Yet three of them were caught by the Duke's company that watched in the plain, and, having been soundly flogged, were set to work as servants in the camp. But the fourth came safe to the hills, and found there Tommasino and Bena; and Tommasino, hearing of Antonio's state, started with Bena and eighteen more to rescue him or die with him. And they fell in with a scouting party of the Duke's, and slew every man of them to the number of five, losing two of their own number; but thus they escaped, there being none left to carry news to the camp; and they rode furiously, and, by the time they came near Baratesta, they were not more than a mile behind Lepardo's company. But Lepardo, when he had detached the six men to watch Antonio, rode on hastily to find the Syndic, and learn from him the meaning of what he had seen; and thus Tommasino, coming opposite to the mouth of the hermit's cave, saw no more than six horses tethered on the river bank, having the Duke's escutcheon wrought on their saddle-cloths. Then he leapt down, and, running to the edge of the bank, saw a man disappearing into the mouth of the cave, dripping wet; and this man was the last of the six who had swum the river, and were now groping their way with great caution along the narrow track that the hermit had made. Now Tommasino understood no more than Lepardo that there was any opening from the cave to the vault, but he thought that the Duke's men did not swim the river for their pleasure, and he bade Bena take five and watch what should happen, while he rode on with the rest.

"If they come out again immediately," he said, "you will have them at a disadvantage; but if they do not come out, go in after them; for I know not what they are doing unless they are seeking my cousin or laying some trap for him."

Then Tommasino rode after Lepardo; and Bena, having given the Duke's men but the briefest space in which to come out again from the cave, prepared to go after them. And the Duke's men were now much alarmed; for the last man told them of the armed men on the bank opposite, and that they did not wear the Duke's badge; so the six retreated up the passage very silently, but they could not find any opening, for it grew darker at every step, and they became much out of heart. Then Bena's men crossed the river and entered the mouth of the cave after them. Thus there was fair likelihood of good fighting both in the passage and by the gate of the vault.

But the Count Antonio, not knowing that any of his band were near, had ceased to hope for his life, and he sat calm and ready, sword in hand, while the hermit withdrew to a corner of the vault, and crouched there muttering his mad answers and questions, and ever and again hailing some one of the dead Peschetti by name as though he saw him. Then suddenly a coffin fell with a loud crash from the top of the heap on to the floor; for the Duke's men had found the opening and were pushing at it with hand and shoulder. Antonio sprang to his feet and left the gate and went and stood ready by the pile of coffins. But again on a sudden came a tumult from beyond the opening; for Bena and his five also were now in the passage, and the foremost of them—who indeed was Bena himself—had come upon the hindmost of the Duke's men, and the six, finding an enemy behind them, pushed yet more fiercely and strenuously against the coffins. And no man in the passage saw any man, it being utterly dark; and they could not use their swords for lack of space, but drew their daggers and thrust fiercely when they felt a man's body near. So in the dark they pushed and wrestled and struggled and stabbed, and the sound of their tumult filled all the vault and spread beyond, being heard outside; and many outside crossed themselves for fear, saying, "Hell is broke loose! God save us!" But at that moment came Lepardo and his company; and he, having leapt from his horse and heard from the Syndic that Antonio was in very truth in the vault, drew his sword and came at the head of his men to the door; and hearing the tumult from within, he cried in scorn, "These are no ghosts!" and himself with his boldest rushed at the door, and they laid hold on the handles of it and wrenched it open. But Antonio, perceiving that the door was wrenched open, and not yet understanding that any of his friends were near, suddenly flung himself prone on the floor by the wall of the vault, behind two of the coffins which the efforts of the Duke's men had dislodged; and there he lay hidden; so that Lepardo, when he rushed in, saw no man, for the corner where the hermit crouched was dark; but the voice of the madman came, saying, "Welcome! Do you bring me another of the Peschetti? He is welcome!" Then the Duke's men, having pushed aside all the coffins save one, came tumbling and scrambling over into the vault, where they found Lepardo and his followers; and hot on their heels came Bena and his five, so that the vault was full of men. And now from outside also came the clatter of hoofs and hoarse cries and the clash of steel; for Tommasino had come, and had fallen with great fury on those of Lepardo's men who were outside and on the Syndic's levies that watched from afar off. And fierce was the battle outside; yet it was fiercer inside, where men fought in a half-light, scarcely knowing with whom they fought, and tripping hither and thither over the coffins of the Peschetti that were strewn about the floor.

Then the Count Antonio arose from where he lay and he cried aloud, "To me, to me! To me, Antonio of Monte Velluto!" and he rushed to the entrance of the vault. Bena, hailing the Count's voice, and cutting down one who barred the way, ran to Antonio in great joy to find him alive and whole. And Antonio came at Lepardo, who stood his onset bravely, although greatly bewildered to find a party of

Antonio's men where he had looked for Antonio alone. And he cried to his men to rally round him, and, keeping his face and his blade towards the Count, began to fall back towards the mouth of the vault, in order to rejoin his men outside; for there also he perceived that there was an enemy. Thus Lepardo fell back, and Antonio pressed on. But, unnoticed by any, the mad hermit now sprang forth from the corner where he had been; and, as Antonio was about to thrust at Lepardo, the hermit caught him by the arm, and with the strength of frenzy drew him back, and thrust himself forward, running even on the point of Lepardo's sword that was ready for Count Antonio; and the sword of Lepardo passed through the breast of the hermit of the vault, and protruded behind his back between his shoulders; and he fell prone on the floor of the vault, crying exultantly, "Death! Thanks be to God, death!" And then and there he died of the thrust that Lepardo gave him. But Antonio with Bena and three more—for two of Bena's five were slain—drove Lepardo and his men back before them, and thus won their way to the gate of the vault, where, to their joy, they found that Tommasino more than held his own; for he had scattered Lepardo's men, and the Syndic's were in full flight, save eight or ten of the old soldiers who had served in Free Companies; and these stood in a group, their swords in their right hands and daggers in the left, determined to die dearly; and the grizzly-haired fellow who had killed Antonio's horse had assumed command of them.

"Here are some fellows worth fighting, my lord," said Bena to Tommasino joyfully. "Let us meet them, my lord, man for man, an equal number of us." For although Bena had killed one man and maimed another in the vault, he saw no reason for staying his hand.

"Aye, Bena," laughed Tommasino. "These fellows deserve to die at the hands of men like us."

But while they prepared to attack, Antonio cried suddenly, "Let them be! There are enough men dead over this matter of Cesare's treasure." And he compelled Tommasino and Bena to come with him, although they were very reluctant; and they seized horses that had belonged to Lepardo's men; and, one of Tommasino's men also being dead, Bena took his horse. Then Antonio said to the men of the Free Companies, "What is your quarrel with me? I do but take what is mine. Go in peace. This Syndic is no master of yours." But the men shook their heads and stood their ground. Then Antonio turned and rode to the entrance of the vault where his band was now besieging Lepardo, and he cried to Lepardo, "Confer with me, sir. You can come forth safely." And Lepardo came out from the vault, having lost there no fewer than five men, and having others wounded; and he was himself wounded in his right arm and could not hold his sword. Then the Count said to him, "Sir, it is no shame for a man to yield when fortune is against him. And I trust that I am one to whom a gentleman may yield without shame. See, the Syndic's men are fled, and yours are scattered, and these men, who stand bravely together, are not enough to resist me."

And Lepardo answered sadly—for he was

very sorry that he had failed to take Antonio—
"Indeed, my lord, we are worsted. For we are
not ten men against one, as I think they should
be who seek to overcome my lord Antonio."

To this Antonio bowed most courteously,
saying, "Nay, it is rather fortune, sir."

And Lepardo said, "Yet we can die, in case
you put unseemly conditions on us, my lord."

"There is no condition save that you fight no
more against me to-day," said Antonio.

"So let it be, my lord," said Lepardo; and to
this the men of the Free Companies also agreed,
and they mingled with Antonio's band, and two
of them joined themselves to Antonio that day,
and were with him henceforward, one being
afterwards slain on Mount Agnino, and the
other preserving his life through all the perils
that beset the Count's company.

Then Antonio went back to the house of
Cesare, and brought forth the body of Cesare,
and, having come to the vault, he caused those
who had been slain to be carried out, and set the
coffins again in decent order, and laid Cesare,
the last of the house, there. But when the

corpse of the hermit was brought out, all marvelled very greatly, and had much compassion for him when they heard from the lips of Count Antonio his pitiful story; and Antonio bestowed out of the moneys that he had from Cesare a large sum that masses might be said for the soul of the hermit. "For of a surety," said the Count, "it was Heaven's will that through his misfortune and the strange madness that came upon him my life should be saved."

These things done, Antonio gathered his band, and, having taken farewell of Lepardo and commended him for the valour of his struggle, prepared to ride back to the hills. And his face was grave, for he was considering earnestly how he should escape the hundred men who lay watching for him in the plain. But while he considered, Tommasino came to him and said, "All Baratesta is ours, cousin. Cannot we get a change of coat, and thus ride with less notice from the Duke's camp?" And Antonio laughed also, and they sent and caught twenty men of Baratesta, grave merchants and petty traders, and among them Bena laid hold of the Syndic, and brought him in his chair to Antonio; and the Count said to the Syndic, "It is ill meddling with the affairs of better men, Master Syndic. Off with that gown of yours!"

And they stripped the Syndic of his gown, and Antonio put on the gown. Thus the Syndic had need very speedily of the new gown which he had contracted to purchase of the lame tailor as the price of the tailor's information. And all Antonio's men clothed themselves like merchants and traders, Antonio in the Syndic's gown taking his place at their head; and thus soberly attired, they rode out soberly from Baratesta, neither Lepardo nor any of his men being able to restrain themselves from laughter to see them go; and most strange of all was Bena, who wore an old man's gown of red cloth trimmed with fur.

It was now noon, and the band rode slowly, for the sun was very hot, and several times they paused to take shelter under clumps of trees, so that the afternoon waned before they came in sight of the Duke's encampment. Soon then they were seen in their turn; and a young officer of the Guard with three men came pricking towards them to learn their business; and Antonio hunched the Syndic's gown about his neck and pulled his cap down over his eyes, and thus received the officer. And the officer was deluded and did not know him, but said, "Is there news, Syndic?"

"Yes, there is news," said Antonio. "The hermit of the vault of the Peschetti is dead at Baratesta."

"I know naught of him," said the officer.

By this time Antonio's men had all crowded round the officer and his companions, hemming them in on every side; and those that watched from the Duke's camp saw the merchants and traders flocking round the officer, and said to themselves, "They are offering wares to him." But Antonio said, "How, sir? You have never heard of the hermit of the vault?"

"I have not, Syndic," said the officer.

"He was a man, sir," said Antonio, "who dwelt with the dead in a vault, and was so enamoured of death, that he greeted it as a man greets a dear friend who has tarried overlong in coming."

"In truth, a strange mood!" cried the officer. "I think this hermit was mad."

"I also think so," said Antonio.

"I cannot doubt of it," cried the officer.

"Then, sir, you are not of his mind?" asked Antonio, smiling. "You would not sleep this night with the dead, nor hold out your hands to death as to a dear friend?"

"By St. Prisian, no," said the young officer with a laugh. "For this world is well enough, Syndic, and I have sundry trifling sins that I would be quit of, before I face another."

"If that be so, sir," said Antonio, "return to him who sent you, and say that the Syndic of Baratesta rides here with a company of friends and that his business is lawful and open to no suspicion." And even as Antonio spoke, every man drew his dagger, and there were three daggers at the heart of the officer and three at the heart of each of the men with him. "For by saying this," continued the Count, fixing his eyes on the officer, "and by no other means can you escape immediate death."

Then the officer looked to right and left,

being very much bewildered; but Tommasino touched him on the arm and said, "You have fallen, sir, into the hands of the Count Antonio. Take an oath to do as he bids you, and save your life." And Antonio took off the Syndic's cap and showed his face; and Bena rolled up the sleeve of his old man's gown and showed the muscles of his arm.

"The Count Antonio!" cried the officer and his men in great dismay.

"Yes; and we are four to one," said Tommasino. "You have no choice, sir, between the oath and immediate death. And it seems to me that you are indeed not of the mind of the hermit of the vault."

But the officer cried, "My honour will not suffer this oath, my lord." And, hearing this, Bena advanced his dagger.

But Antonio smiled again and said, "Then I will not force it on you, sir. But this much I must force on you—to swear to abide here for half-an-hour, and during that time to send no word and make no sign to your camp."

To this the officer, having no choice between

it and death, agreed; and Antonio, leaving him, rode forward softly; and, riding softly, he passed within half-a-mile of the Duke's encampment. But at this moment the officer, seeing Antonio far away, broke his oath, and shouted loudly, "It is Antonio of Monte Velluto;" and set spurs to his horse. Then Antonio's brow grew dark and he said, "Ride on swiftly, all of you, to the hills, and leave me here."

"My lord!" said Tommasino, beseeching him.

"Ride on!" said Antonio sternly. "Ride at a gallop. You will draw them off from me."

And they dared not disobey him, but all rode on. And now there was a stir in the Duke's camp, men running for their arms and their horses. But Antonio's band set themselves to a gallop, making straight for the hills; and the commander of the Duke's Guard did not know what to make of the matter; for he had heard the officer cry "Antonio," but did not understand what he meant; therefore there was a short delay before the pursuit after the band was afoot; and the band thus gained an advantage, and Antonio turned away, saying, "It is enough. They will come safe to the hills."

But he himself drew his sword and set spurs to his horse, and he rode towards where the young officer was. And at first the officer came boldly to meet him; then he wavered, and his cheek went pale; and he said to the men who rode with him, "We are four to one."

"But one of them answered, "Four to two, sir."

"What do you mean?" cried the officer. "I see none coming towards us but Count Antonio himself."

"Is not God also against oath-breakers?" said the fellow, and he looked at his comrades. And they nodded their heads to him; for they were afraid to fight by the side of a man who had broken his oath. Moreover the figure of the Count was very terrible; and the three turned aside and left the young officer alone.

Now by this time the whole of the Duke's encampment was astir; but they followed not after Antonio, but after Tommasino and the rest of the band; for they did not know Antonio in the Syndic's gown. Thus the young officer was left alone to meet Antonio; and when he saw this his heart failed him and his courage sank, and he dared not await Antonio, but he turned and set spurs to his horse, and fled away from Antonio across the plain. And Antonio pursued after him, and was now very near upon him; so that the officer saw that he would soon be overtaken, and the reins fell from his hand and he sat on his horse like a man smitten with a palsy, shaking and trembling: and his horse, being unguided, stumbled as it went, and the officer fell off from it; and he lay very still on the ground. Then Count Antonio came up where the officer was, and sat on his horse, holding his drawn sword in his hand; and in an instant the officer began to raise himself; and, when he stood up, he saw Antonio with his sword drawn. And Antonio said, "Shall men without honour live?"

Then the officer gazed into the eyes of the Count Antonio; and the sweat burst forth on his forehead. A sudden strange choking cry came from him; he dropped his sword from his hand, and with both hands he suddenly clasped his heart, uttering now a great cry of pain and having his face wrung with agony. Thus he stood for an instant, clutching his heart with both his hands, his mouth twisted fearfully, and then he dropped on to the ground and lay still. And the Count Antonio sheathed his sword, and bared his head, saying, "It is not my sword, but God's."

And he turned and put his horse to a gallop and rode away, not seeking to pass the Duke's encampment, but directing his way towards the village of Rilano; and there he found shelter in the house of a friend for some hours, and when night fell, made his way safely back to the hills, and found that the Duke's men had abandoned the pursuit of his company and that all of them were alive and safe.

But when they came to take up the young officer who had been false to his oath, he was dead; whether from fright at the aspect of Count Antonio and the imminent doom with which he was threatened, or by some immediate judgment of Heaven, I know not. For very various are the dealings of God with man.

For one crime He will slay and tarry not, and so, perchance, was it meted out to that officer; but with another man His way is different, and He suffers him to live long days, mindful of his sin, in self-hatred and self-scorn, and will not send him the relief of death, how much soever the wretch may pray for it. Thus it was that God dealt with the hermit of the vault of the Peschetti, who did not find death till he had sought it for twenty-and-three years. I doubt not that in all there is purpose; even as was shown in the manner wherein the hermit, being himself bound and tied to a miserable life, was an instrument in saving the life of Count Antonio.

CHAPTER VII.

COUNT ANTONIO AND THE LADY OF RILANO.

From the lips of Tommasino himself, who was cousin to Count Antonio, greatly loved by him, and partaker of all his enterprises during the time of his sojourn as an outlaw in the hills, this, the story of the Lady of Rilano, came to my venerable brother in Christ, Niccolo; and the same Niccolo, being a very old man, told it to me, so that I know that the story is true and every part of it, and tread here not on the doubtful ground of legend, but on the firm rock of the word of honest men. There is indeed one thing doubtful, Tommasino himself being unable to know the verity of it; yet that one thing is of small moment, for it is no more than whether the lady came first to Duke Valentine, offering her aid, or whether the Duke, who since the affair of the sacred bones had been ever active in laying schemes against Antonio, cast his eyes on the lady, and, perceiving that she was very fair and likely to serve his turn, sent for her, and persuaded her by gifts and by the promise of a great marriage to take the task in hand.

Be that as it may, it is certain that in the fourth year of Count Antonio's outlawry, the Lady Venusta came from Rilano, where she dwelt, and talked alone with the Duke in his cabinet; so that men (and women with greater urgency) asked what His Highness did to take such a one into his counsels; for he had himself forbidden her to live in the city and constrained her to abide in her house at Rilano, by reason of reports touching her fair fame. Nor did she then stay in Firmola, but, having had audience of the Duke, returned straightway to Rilano, and for the space of three weeks rested there; and the Duke told nothing to his lords of what had passed between him and the lady, while the Count Antonio and his friends knew not so much as that the Duke had held conference with the lady; for great penalties had been decreed against any man who sent word to Antonio of what passed in Firmola, and the pikemen kept strict guard on all who left or entered the city, so that it was rather like a town besieged than the chief place of a peaceful realm.

Now at this time, considering that his hiding-place was too well known to the Lord Lorenzo and certain of the Duke's Guard, Count Antonio descended from the hills by night, and, having crossed the plain, carrying all his equipment with him, mounted again into the heights of Mount Agnino and pitched his camp in and about a certain cave, which is protected on two sides by high rocks and on the third by the steep banks of a river, and can be approached by one path only. This cave was known to the Duke, but he could not force it without great loss, so that Antonio was well nigh as safe as when his hiding-place had been unknown; and yet he was nearer by half to the city, and but seven miles as a bird flies from the village of Rilano where the Lady Venusta dwelt; although to one who travelled by the only path that a man could go upright on his feet the distance was hard on eleven miles. But no other place was so near, and from Rilano Antonio drew the better part of the provisions and stores of which he had need, procuring them secretly from the people, who were very strictly enjoined by the Duke to furnish him with nothing under pain of forfeiture of all their goods.

Yet one day, when the man they called Bena and a dozen more rode in the evening through Rilano, returning towards the cave, the maid-servant of Venusta met them, and, with her, men bearing a great cask of fine wine, and the maid-servant said to Bena, "My mistress bids you drink; for good men should not suffer thirst."

But Bena answered her, asking, "Do you know who we are?"

"Aye, I know, and my lady knows," said the girl. "But my lady says that if she must live at Rilano, then she will do what she pleases in Rilano."

Bena and his men looked at one another, for they knew of His Highness's proclamation, but the day having been hot, they being weary, the wine seeming good, and a woman knowing her own business best, at last they drank heartily, and, rendering much thanks, rode on and told Tommasino what had been done. And Tommasino having told Antonio, the Count was angry with Bena, saying that his gluttony would bring trouble on the Lady Venusta.

"She should not tempt a man," said Bena sullenly.

All these things happened on the second day of the week; and on the fourth, towards evening, as Antonio and Tommasino sat in front of the cave, they saw coming towards them one of the band named Luigi, a big fellow who had done good service and was also a merry jovial man that took the lead in good-fellowship. And in his arms Luigi bore the Lady Venusta. Her gown was dishevelled and torn, and the velvet shoes on her feet were cut almost to shreds, and she lay back in Luigi's arms, pale and exhausted. Luigi came and set her down gently before Antonio, saying, "My lord, three miles from here, in the steepest and roughest part of the way, I found this lady sunk on the ground and half-swooning: when I raised her and asked how she came where she was, and in such a plight, she could answer nothing save, 'Count Antonio! Carry me to Count Antonio!' So I have brought her in obedience to her request."

As Luigi ended, Venusta opened her eyes, and, rising to her knees, held out her hands in supplication, saying, "Protect me, my lord, protect me. For the Duke has sent me word that to-morrow night he will burn my house and all that it holds, and will take me and lodge me in prison, and so use me there that I may know what befalls those who give aid to traitors. And all this comes upon me, my lord, because I gave a draught of wine to your men when they were thirsty."

"I feared this thing," said Antonio, "and deeply I grieve at it. But I am loth to go in open war against the Duke; moreover in the plain he would be too strong for me. What then can I do? For here is no place in which a lady, the more if she be alone and unattended, can be lodged with seemliness."

"If the choice be between this and a prison——" said Venusta with a faint sorrowful smile.

"Yet it might be that I could convey you beyond His Highness's power," pursued Antonio. "But I fear you could not travel far to-night."

"Indeed I am weary even to death," moaned Venusta.

"There is nothing for it but that to-night at least she rest here," said Antonio to Tommasino.

Tommasino frowned. "When woman comes in," said he behind the screen of his hand, "safety flies out."

"Better fly safety than courtesy and kindness, cousin," said Count Antonio, and Tommasino ceased to dissuade him, although he was uneasy concerning the coming of Venusta.

That night, therefore, all made their camp outside, and gave the cave to Venusta for her use, having made a curtain of green boughs across its mouth. But again the next day Venusta was too sick for travel; nay, she seemed very sick, and she prayed Luigi to go to Rilano and seek a physician; and Luigi, Antonio having granted him permission, went, and returned saying that no physician dared come in face of His Highness's proclamation; but the truth was that Luigi was in the pay of Venusta and of the Duke, and had sought by his journey not a physician, but means of informing the Duke how Venusta had sped, and of seeking counsel from him as to what should next be done. And that day and for four days more Venusta abode in the cave, protesting that she could not travel; and Antonio used her with great courtesy, above all when he heard that the Duke, having stayed to muster all his force for fear of Antonio, had at length appointed the next day for the burning of her house at Rilano and the carrying off of all her goods. These tidings he gave her, and though he spoke gently, she fell at once into great distress, declaring that she had not believed the Duke would carry out his purpose, and weeping for her jewels and prized possessions which were in the house.

Now Count Antonio, though no true man could call him fool, had yet a simplicity nobler it may be than the suspicious wisdom of those who, reading other hearts by their own, count all men rogues and all women wanton: and when he saw the lady weeping for the trinkets and her loved toys and trifles, he said, "Nay, though I cannot meet the Duke face to face, yet I will ride now and come there before him, and bring what you value most from the house."

"You will be taken," said she, and she gazed at him with timid admiring eyes. "I had rather a thousand times lose the jewels than that you should run into danger, my lord. For I owe to you liberty, and perhaps life."

"I will leave Tommasino to guard you and ride at once," and Antonio rose to his feet, smiling at her for her foolish fears.

Then a thing that seemed strange happened. For Antonio gave a sudden cry of pain. And behold, he had set his foot on the point of a dagger that was on the ground near to the Lady Venusta; and the dagger ran deep into his foot, for it was resting on a stone and the point sloped upwards, so that he trod full and with all his weight on the point; and he sank back on the ground with the dagger in his foot. How came the dagger there? How came it to rest against the stone? None could tell then, though it seems plain to him that considers now. None then thought that the lady who fled to Antonio as though he were her lover, and lavished tears and sighs on him, had placed it there. Nor that honest Luigi, who made such moan of his carelessness in dropping his poniard, had taken more pains over the losing of his weapon than most men over the preservation of theirs. Luigi cursed himself, and the lady cried out on fate; and Count Antonio consoled both of them, saying that the wound would soon be well, and that it was too light a matter for a lady to dim her bright eyes for the sake of it.

Yet light as the matter was, it was enough for Venusta's purpose and for the scheme of Duke Valentine. For Count Antonio could neither mount his horse nor go afoot to Venusta's house in Rilano; and, if the jewels were to be saved and the lady's tears dried (mightily, she declared with pretty self-reproach, was she ashamed to think of the jewels beside Antonio's hurt, but yet they were dear to her), then Tommasino must go in his place to Rilano.

"And take all save Bena and two more," said Antonio. "For the Duke will not come here if he goes to Rilano."

"I," said Bena, "am neither nurse nor physician nor woman. Let Martolo stay; he says there is already too much blood on his conscience; and let me go, for there is not so much as I could bear on mine, and maybe we shall have a chance of an encounter with the foreguard of the Duke."

But Venusta said to Antonio, "Let both of these men go, and let Luigi stay. For he is a clever fellow, and will aid me in tending your wound."

"So be it," said Antonio. "Let Luigi and the two youngest stay; and do the rest of you go, and return as speedily as you may. And the Lady Venusta shall, of her great goodness, dress my wound, which pains me more than such a trifle should."

Thus the whole band, saving Luigi and two youths, rode off early in the morning with Tommasino, their intent being to reach Rilano and get clear of it again before the Duke came thither from the city; and Venusta sent no message to the Duke, seeing that all had fallen out most prosperously and as had been arranged between them. For the Duke was not in truth minded to go at all to Rilano; but at earliest dawn, before Tommasino had set forth, the Lord Lorenzo left the city with a hundred pikemen; more he would not take, fearing to be delayed if his troop were too large; and he made a great circuit, avoiding Rilano and the country adjacent to it. So that by mid-day Tommasino was come with thirty-and-four men (the whole strength of the band except the three with Antonio) to Rilano, and, meeting with no resistance, entered Venusta's house, and took all that was precious in it, and loaded their horses with the rich tapestries and the choicest of the furnishings; and then, having regaled themselves with good cheer, started in the afternoon to ride back to the cave, Tommasino and Bena grumbling to one another because they had chanced on no fighting, but not daring to tarry by reason of Antonio's orders.

But their lamentations were without need; for when they came to the pass of Mount

Agnino, there at the entrance of the road which led up to the cave, by the side of the river, was encamped a force of eighty pikemen under the Lieutenant of the Guard. Thus skilfully had the Lord Lorenzo performed his duty, and cut off Tommasino and his company from all access to the cave; and now he himself was gone with twenty men up the mountain path, to take Antonio according to the scheme of the Duke and the Lady Venusta. But Bena and Tommasino were sore aghast, and said to one another, "There is treachery. What are we to do?" For the eighty of the Duke's men were posted strongly, and it was a great hazard to attack them. Yet this risk they would have run, for they were ready rather to die than to sit there idle while Antonio was taken; and in all likelihood they would have died, had the Lieutenant obeyed the orders which Lorenzo had given him and rested where he was, covered by the hill and the river. But the Lieutenant was a young man, of hot temper and impetuous, and to his mistaken pride it seemed as though it were cowardice for eighty men to shrink from attacking thirty-and-five, and for the Duke's Guards to play for advantage in a contest with a band of robbers. Moreover Tommasino's men taunted his men, crying to them to come down and fight like men in the open. Therefore, counting on a sure victory and the pardon it would gain, about three o'clock in the afternoon he cried, "Let us have at these rascals!" and to Tommasino's great joy, his troop remounted their horses and made ready to charge from their position. Then Tommasino said, "We are all ready to face the enemy for my lord and cousin's sake. But I have need now of those who will run away for his sake."

Then he laid his plans that when the Lieutenant's troop charged, his men should not stand their ground. And five men he placed on one extremity of his line, Bena at their head; and four others with himself he posted at the other extremity; also he spread out his line very wide, so that it stretched on either side beyond the line of the Lieutenant. And he bade the twenty-and-five in the centre not abide the onset, but turn and flee at a gallop, trusting to the speed of their horses for escape. And he made them fling away all that they had brought from the Lady Venusta's house, that they might ride the lighter.

"And I pray God," said he, "that you will escape alive; but if you do not, it is only what your oath to my lord constrains you to. But you and I, Bena, with our men, will ride, not back towards the plain, but on towards the hills, and it may be that we shall thus get ahead of the Lieutenant; and once we are ahead of him in the hilly ground, he will not catch us before we come to the cave."

"Unless," began Bena, "there be another party——"

"Hist!" said Tommasino, and he whispered to Bena, "They will fear if they hear all."

Then the Duke's men came forth, and it fell out as Tommasino had planned; for the body of the Duke's men, when they saw Tommasino's rank broken and his band flying, set up a great shout of scorn and triumph, and dug spurs into their horses and pursued the runaways. And the runaways rode at their top speed, and, having come nearly to Rilano without being caught, they were three of them overtaken and captured by the well at the entrance to the village; but the rest, wheeling to the right, dashed across the plain, making for Antonio's old hiding-place; and, having lost two more of their number whose horses failed, and having slain four of the Guard who pursued incautiously ahead of the rest, they reached the spurs of the hills, and there scattered, every man by himself, and found refuge, some in the woods, some in shepherds' huts; so they came off with their lives. But the men with Tommasino and Bena had ridden straight for the hill-road, and had passed the Lieutenant before he apprehended Tommasino's scheme. Then he cried aloud to his men, and eight of them, hearing him, checked their horses, but could not understand what he desired of them till he cried aloud again, and pointed with his hand towards where the ten, Tommasino leading and Bena in the rear, had gained the hill-road and were riding up it as swiftly as their horses could mount. Then the Lieutenant, cursing his own folly, gathered them, and they rode after Tommasino and Bena.

"Be of good heart," said the Lieutenant. "They are between us and the company of my Lord Lorenzo."

Yet though he said this, his mind was not at ease; for the horses of his men, being unaccustomed to the hills, could not mount the road as did the sure-footed mountain-horses ridden by Tommasino's company, and the space widened between them; and at last Tommasino's company disappeared from sight, at the point where the track turned sharp to the left, round a great jutting rock that stood across the way and left room for but three men to ride abreast between river and rock. Then the Lieutenant drew rein and took counsel with his men, for he feared that Tommasino would wait for him behind the jutting rock and dash out on his flank as he rode round. Therefore for a while he considered, and a while longer he allowed for the breathing of the horses; and then with great caution rode on towards the jutting rock, which lay about the half of a mile from him. And when he came near it, he and his men heard a voice cry, "Quiet, quiet! They are close now!"

"They will dash at us as we go round," said the Lieutenant.

"And we can go no more than three together," said one of the guards.

"Are you all ready?" said the voice behind the cliff, in accents that but just reached round the rock. "Not a sound, for your lives!" Yet a sound there was, as of a jingling bit, and then again an angry, "Curse you, you clumsy fool, be still." And then all was still.

"They are ready for us now," whispered a guard, with an uneasy smile.

"I will go," said the Lieutenant. "Which two of you will lead the way with me?"

But the men grumbled, saying, "It is the way to death that you ask us to lead, sir."

Then the Lieutenant drew his men back, and as they retreated they made a noise great hoping to make Tommasino think they were gone. And, having thus withdrawn some five hundred paces, they rested in utter quiet for half an hour. And it was then late afternoon. And the Lieutenant said, "I will go first alone, and in all likelihood I shall be slain; but do you follow immediately after me and avenge my death." And this they, being ashamed for their first refusal, promised to do. Then the Lieutenant rode softly forward till he came within twenty yards of the rock, and he clapped spurs to his horse and shouted, and, followed close by his men crying, "For God and our Duke!" charged round the jutting rock.

And behold, on the other side of it was not a man! And of Tommasino and his company naught was to be seen—for they had used the last hour to put a great distance between them and their pursuers—save that away, far up the road, in the waning light of the sun, was to be dimly perceived the figure of a man on horseback, who waved his hat to them and, turning, was in an instant lost to view. And this man was Bena, who, by himself and without a blow, had held the passage of the jutting rock for hard on an hour, and thus given time to Tommasino to ride on and come upon the rear of Lorenzo's company before the Lieutenant and his men could hem them in on the other side.

Thus had the day worn to evening, and long had the day seemed to Antonio, who sat before the mouth of the cave, with Venusta by his side. All day they had sat thus alone, for Luigi and the two youths had gone to set snares in the wood behind the cave—or such was the pretext Luigi made; and Antonio had let them go, charging them to keep in earshot. As the long day passed, Antonio, seeking to entertain the lady and find amusement for her through the hours, began to recount to her all that he had done, how he had seized the Sacred Bones, the manner of his difference with the Abbot of St. Prisian, and much else. But of the killing of Duke Paul he would not speak; nor did he speak of his love for Lucia till Venusta pressed him, making parade of great sympathy for him. But when he had set his tongue to the task, he grew eloquent, his eyes gleamed and his cheek flushed, and he spoke in the low reverent voice that a true lover uses when he speaks of his mistress, as though his wonted accents were too common and mean for her name. And Venusta sat listening, casting now and again a look at him out of her deep eyes, and finding his eyes never on hers but filled with the fancied vision of Lucia. And at last, growing impatient with him, she broke out petulantly, "Is this girl, then, different from all others, that you speak of her as though she were a goddess?"

"I would not have spoken of her but that you pressed me," laughed Antonio. "Yet in my eyes she is a goddess, as every maid should be to her lover."

Venusta caught a twig from the ground and broke it sharp across. "Boys' talk!" said she, and flung the broken twig away.

Antonio laughed gently, and leant back, resting on the rock. "May be," said he. "Yet is there none who talks boys' talk for you?"

"I love men," said she, "not boys. And if I were a man I think I would love a woman, not a goddess."

"It is Heaven's chance, I doubt not," said Antonio, laughing again. "Had you and I chanced to love, we should not have quarrelled with the boys' talk nor at the name of goddess."

She flushed suddenly and bit her lip, but she answered in raillery, "Indeed had it been so, a marvel of a lover I should have had! For you have not seen your mistress for many, many months, and yet you are faithful to her. Are you not, my lord?"

"Small credit not to wander where you love to rest," said Antonio.

"And yet youth goes in waiting, and delights missed come not again," said she, leaning towards him with a light in her eyes, and scanning his fair hair and bronzed cheek, his broad shoulders and the sinewy hands that nursed his knee.

"It may well be that they will not come to me," he said. "For the Duke has a halter ready for my throat, if by force or guile he can take me."

She started at these words, searching his face; but he was calm and innocent of any hidden meaning. She forced a laugh as she said, twisting a curl of her hair round her finger,

"The more reason to waste no time, my Lord Antonio."

Antonio shook his head and said lightly, "But I think he cannot take me by force, and I know of no man in all the Duchy that would betray me to a shameful death."

"And of no woman?" she asked, glancing at him from under drooping lashes.

"No, for I have wronged none; and women are not cruel."

"Yet there may be some, my lord, who call you cruel and therefore would be cruel in vengeance. A lover faithful as you can have but one friend among women."

"I know of none such," he laughed. "And surely the vengeance would be too great for the offence, if there were such."

"Nay, I know not that," said Venusta, frowning.

"I would trust myself to any woman, even though the Duke offered her great rewards, aye, as readily as I put faith in Lucia herself, or in you."

"You couple me with her?"

"In that matter most readily," said Antonio.

"But in nothing else?" she asked, flushing again in anger, for still his eyes were distant, and he turned them never on her.

"You must pardon me," he said. "My eyes are blinded."

For a moment she sat silent; then she said in a low voice, "But blind eyes have learned to see before now, my lord."

Then Antonio set his eyes on her; and now she could not meet them, but turned her burning face away. For her soul was in tumult, and she knew not now whether she loved or hated him, nor whether she would save or still betray him. And the trust he had in her gnawed her guilty heart. So that a sudden passion seized her, and she caught Antonio by the arm, crying, "But if a woman held your life in her hand and asked your love as its price, Antonio?"

"Such a thing could not be," said he, wondering.

"Nay, but it might. And if it were?"

And Antonio, marvelling more and more at

her vehemence, answered, "Love is dear, and honour is dear; but we of Monte Velluto hold life of no great price."

"Yet it is a fearful and shameful thing to hang from the city wall."

"There are worse things," said he. "But indeed I count not to do it;" and he laughed again.

Venusta sprang to her feet and paced the space between the cave and the river bank with restless steps. Once she flung her hands above her head and clasped them; then, holding them clasped in front of her, she stood by Antonio and bent over him, till her hair, falling forward as she stooped, brushed his forehead and mingled with his fair locks; and she breathed softly his name, "Antonio, Antonio!" At this he looked up with a great start, stretching up his hand as though to check her; but he said nothing. And she, suddenly sobbing, fell on her knees by him; yet, as suddenly, she ceased to sob, and a smile came on her lips, and she leant towards him, saying again, "Antonio."

"I pray you, I pray you," said he, seeking to stay her courteously.

Then, careless of her secret, she flashed out in wrath, "Ah, you scorn me, my lord! You care nothing for me. I am dirt to you. Yet I hold your life in my hand!" And then in an instant she grew again softened, beseeching, "Am I so hideous, dear lord, that death is better than my love? For if you will love me, I will save you."

"I know not how my life is in your hands," said he, glad to catch at that and leave the rest of what Venusta said.

"Is there any path that leads higher up into the mountains?" she asked.

"Yes, there is one," said he; "but if need came now, I could not climb it with this wounded foot of mine."

"Luigi and the young men could carry you?"

"Yes; but what need? Tommasino and the band will return soon."

But she caught him by the hand, crying, "Rise, rise; call the men and let them carry you. Come, there is no time for lingering. And if I save you, my Lord Antonio——?" And a yearning question sounded in her voice.

"If you save me a thousand times, I can do nothing else than pray you spare me what is more painful than death to me," said he, looking away from her and being himself in great confusion.

"Come, come," she cried. "Call them! Perhaps some day——! Call them, Antonio."

But as she spoke, before Antonio could call, there came a loud cry from the wood behind the cave, the cry of a man in some great strait. Antonio's hand flew to his sword, and he rose to his feet, and stood leaning on his sword. Then he cried aloud to Luigi. And in a moment Luigi and one of the youths came running; and Luigi, casting one glance at Venusta, said breathlessly, "My lord, Jacopo's foot slipped, and the poor fellow has fallen down a precipice thirty feet deep on to the rocks below, and we fear that he is sore hurt."

Venusta sprang a step forward, for she suspected (what the truth was) that Luigi himself had aided the slipping of Jacopo's foot by a sudden lurch against him; but she said nothing, and Antonio bade Luigi go quick and look after Jacopo, and take the other youth with him.

"But we shall leave you unguarded, my lord," said Luigi with a cunning show of solicitude.

"I am in no present danger, and the youth may be dying. Go speedily," said Antonio.

Luigi turned, and with the other youth (Tommasino told Niccolo his name, but Niccolo had forgotten it) rushed off; and even as he went, Venusta cried, "It is a lie! You yourself brought it about!" But Luigi did not hear her, and Antonio, left again alone, asked her, "What mean you?"

"Nay, I mean naught," said she, affrighted, and, when faced by his inquiring eyes, not daring to confess her treachery.

"I hope the lad is not killed," said Antonio.

"I care not for a thousand lads. Think of yourself, my lord!" And planning to rouse Antonio without betraying herself, she said, "I distrust this man Luigi. Is he faithful? The Duke can offer great rewards."

"He has served me well. I have no reason to mistrust him," said Antonio.

"Ah, you trust every one!" she cried in passion and in scorn of his simplicity. "You trust Luigi! You trust me!"

"Why not?" said he. "But indeed now I have no choice. For they cannot carry both Jacopo and me up the path."

"Jacopo! You would stay for Jacopo?" she flashed out fiercely.

"If nothing else, yet my oath would bind me not to leave him while he lives. For we of the band are all bound to one another as brethren by an oath, and it would look ill if I, for whom they all have given much, were the first to break the oath. So here I am, and here I must stay," and Antonio ended smiling, and, his foot hurting him while he stood, sat down again and rested against the rock.

It was now late, and evening fell; and Venusta knew that the Duke's men should soon be upon them. And she sat down near Antonio and buried her face in her hands, and she wept. For Antonio had so won on her by his honour and his gentleness, and most of all by his loyal clinging to the poor boy Jacopo, that she could not think of her treachery without loathing and horror. Yet she dared not tell him; that now seemed worse to her than death. And while they sat thus, Luigi came and told Antonio that the youth was sore hurt and that they could not lift him.

"Then stay by him," said Antonio. "I need nothing."

And Luigi bowed, and, turning, went back to the other youth, and bade him stay by Jacopo, while he went by Antonio's orders to seek for some one to aid in carrying him. "I may chance," said he, "to find some shepherds." So he went, not to seek shepherds, but to seek the Duke's men, and tell them that they might safely come upon Antonio, for he had now none to guard him.

Then Antonio said to Venusta, "Why do you sit and weep?"

For he thought that she wept because he had scorned the love in which her words declared her to hold him, and he was sorry. But she made no answer.

And he went on, "I pray you, do not weep. For think not that I am blind to your beauty or to the sweet kindness which you have bestowed upon me. And in all things that I may, I will truly and faithfully serve you to my death."

Then she raised her head and she said, "That will not be long, Antonio."

"I know not, but for so long as it may be," said he.

"It will not be long," she said again, and burst into quick passionate sobs, that shook her and left her at last breathless and exhausted.

Antonio looked at her for a while and said, "There is something that you do not tell me. Yet if it be anything that causes you pain or shame, you may tell me as readily as you would any man. For I am not a hard man, and I have many things on my own conscience that forbid me to judge harshly of another."

She raised her head and she lifted her hand into the air. The stillness of evening had fallen, and a light wind blew up from the plain. There seemed no sound save from the flowing of the river and the gentle rustle of the trees.

"Hark!" said she. "Hark! hark!" and with every repetition of the word her voice rose till it ended in a cry of terror.

Antonio set his hand to his ear and listened intently. "It is the sound of men's feet on the rocky path," said he, smiling. "Tommasino returns, and I doubt not that he brings your jewels with him. Will you not give him a smiling welcome? Aye, and to me also your smiles would be welcome. For your weeping melts my heart, and the dimness of your eyes is like a cloud across the sun."

Venusta's sobs had ceased, and she looked at Antonio with a face calm, white, and set. "It is not the Lord Tommasino," she said. "The men you hear are the Duke's men;" and then and there she told him the whole. Yet she spoke as though neither he nor any other were there, but as though she rehearsed for her own ear some lesson that she had learnt; so lifeless and monotonous was her voice as it related the shameful thing. And at last she ended saying,

"Thus in an hour you will be dead, or captured and held for a worse death. It is I who have done it." And she bent her head again to meet her hands; yet she did not cover her face, but rested her chin on her hands, and her eyes were fixed immovably on Count Antonio.

For the space of a minute or two he sat silent. Then he said, "I fear, then, that Tommasino and the rest have had a fight against great odds. But they are stout fellows, Tommasino, and old Bena, and the rest. I hope it is well with them." Then, after a pause, he went on, "Yes, the sound of the steps comes nearer. They will be here before long now. But I had not thought it of Luigi. The rogue! I trust they will not find the two lads."

Venusta sat silent, waiting for him to reproach her. He read her thought on her face, and he smiled at her, and said to her, "Go and meet them; or go, if you will, away up the path. For you should not be here when the end comes."

Then she flung herself at his feet, asking forgiveness, but finding no word for her prayer.

"Aye, aye," said he gently. "But of God you must ask it in prayers and good deeds." And he dragged himself to the cave and set himself with his back against the rock and his face towards the path along which the Duke's men must come. And he called again to Venusta, saying, "I pray you, do not stay here." But she heeded him not, but sat again on the ground, her chin resting on her hands and her eyes on his.

"Hark, they are near now!" said he. And he looked round at sky and trees, and at the rippling swift river, and at the long dark shadows of the hills; and he listened to the faint sounds of the birds and living creatures in the wood. And a great lust of life came over him, and for a moment his lip quivered and his head fell; he was very loth to die. Yet soon he smiled again and raised his head, and so leant easily against the rock.

Now the Lord Lorenzo and his twenty men, conceiving that the Lieutenant of the Guard could without difficulty hold Tommasino, had come along leisurely, desiring to be in good order and not weary when they met Antonio;

for they feared him. And thus it was evening when they came near the cave and halted a moment to make their plans; and here Luigi met them and told them how Antonio was alone and unguarded. But Lorenzo desired, if it were possible, to take Antonio alive and carry him alive to the Duke, knowing that thus he would win His Highness's greatest thanks. And while they talked of how this might best be effected, they in their turn heard the sound of men coming up the road, this sound being made by Tommasino, Bena, and their party, who had ridden as fast as the weariness of their horses let them. But because they had ridden fast, their horses were foundered, and they had dismounted, and were now coming on foot; and Lorenzo heard them coming just as he also had decided to go forward on foot, and had caused the horses to be led into the wood and tethered there. And he asked, "Who are these?"

Then one of his men, a skilled woodsman and hunter, listening, answered, "They are short of a dozen, my lord. They must be come with tidings from the Lieutenant of the Guard. For they would be more if the Lieutenant came himself, or if by chance Tommasino's band had eluded him."

"Come," said Lorenzo. "The capture of the Count must be ours, not theirs. Let us go forward without delay."

Thus Lorenzo and his men pushed on; and but the half of a mile behind came Tommasino and his; and again, three or four miles behind them, came the Lieutenant and his; and all these companies were pressing on towards the cave where Antonio and Venusta were. But Tommasino's men still marched the quicker, and they gained on Lorenzo, while the Lieutenant did not gain on them; yet by reason of the unceasing windings of the way, as it twisted round rocks and skirted precipices, they did not come in sight of Lorenzo, nor did he see them; indeed he thought now of nothing but of coming first on Antonio, and of securing the glory of taking him before the Lieutenant came up. And Tommasino, drawing near the cave, gave his men orders to walk very silently; for he hoped to surprise Lorenzo unawares. Thus, as the sun sank out of sight, Lorenzo came to the cave and to the open space between it and the river, and beheld Antonio standing with his back against the rock and his drawn sword in his hand, and Venusta crouched on the ground some paces away. When Venusta saw Lorenzo, she gave a sharp stifled cry, but did not move: Antonio smiled, and drew himself to his full height.

"Your tricks have served you well, my lord," he said. "Here I am alone and crippled."

"Then yield yourself," said Lorenzo. "We are twenty to one."

"I will not yield," said Antonio. "I can die here as well as at Firmola, and a thrust is better than a noose."

Then Lorenzo, being a gentleman of high spirit and courage, waved his men back; and they stood still ten paces off, watching intently as Lorenzo advanced towards Antonio, for, though Antonio was lamed, yet they looked to see fine fighting. And Lorenzo advanced towards Antonio, and said again, "Yield yourself, my lord."

"I will not yield," said Antonio again.

At this instant the woodsman who was with Lorenzo raised his hand to his ear and listened for a moment; but Tommasino came softly, and the woodsman was deceived. "It is but leaves," he said, and turned again to watch Lorenzo. And that lord now sprang fiercely on Antonio and the swords crossed. And as they crossed, Venusta crawled on her knees nearer, and as the swords played, nearer still she came, none noticing her, till at length she was within three yards of Lorenzo. He now was pressing Antonio hard, for the Count was in great pain from his foot, and as often as he was compelled to rest his weight on it, it came near to failing him, nor could he follow up any advantage he might gain against Lorenzo. Thus passed three or four minutes in the encounter. And the woodsman cried, "Hark! Here comes the Lieutenant. Quick, my lord, or you lose half the glory!" Then Lorenzo sprang afresh on Antonio. Yet as he sprang, another sprang also; and as that other sprang there rose a shout from Lorenzo's men; yet they did not rush to aid in the capture of Antonio, but turned themselves round. For Bena, with Tommasino at his heels, had shot among them like a stone hurled from a catapult; and this man Bena was a great fighter; and now he was all aflame with love and fear for Count Antonio. And he crashed through their ranks, and split the head of the woodsman with the heavy sword he carried; and thus he came to Lorenzo. But there in amazement he stood still. For Antonio and Lorenzo had dropped their points and fought no more; but both stood with their eyes on the slim figure of a girl that lay on the ground between them; and blood was pouring from a wound in her breast, and she moaned softly. And while the rest fought fiercely, these three stood looking on the girl; and Lorenzo looked also on his sword, which was dyed three inches up the blade. For as he thrust most fiercely at Antonio, Venusta had sprung at him with the spring of a young tiger, a dagger flashing in her hand, and in the instinct that sudden danger brings he had turned his blade against her; and the point of it was deep in her breast before he drew it back with horror and a cry of "Heavens! I have killed her!" And she fell full on the ground at the feet of Count Antonio, who had stood motionless in astonishment, with his sword in rest.

Now the stillness and secrecy of Tommasino's approach had served him well, for he had come upon Lorenzo's men when they had no thought of an enemy, but stood crowded together, shoulder to shoulder; and several of them were slain and more hurt before they could use their swords to any purpose; but Tommasino's men had fallen on them with great fury, and had broken through them even as Bena had, and, getting above them, were now, step by step, driving them down the path, and formed a rampart between them and the three who stood by the dying lady. And when Bena perceived this advantage, wasting little thought on Venusta (he was a hard man, this Bena), he cried to Antonio, "Leave him to me, my lord. We have him sure!" and in an instant he would have sprung at Lorenzo, who, finding himself between two enemies, knew that his state was perilous, but was yet minded to defend himself. But Antonio suddenly cried in a loud voice, "Stay!"

and arrested by his voice, all stood still, Lorenzo where he was, Tommasino and his men at the top of the path, and the Guards just below them. And Antonio, leaning on his sword, stepped a pace forward and said to Lorenzo, "My lord, the dice have fallen against you. But I would not fight over this lady's body. The truth of all she did I know, yet she has at the last died that I might live. See, my men are between you and your men."

"It is the hazard of war," said Lorenzo.

"Aye," said Bena. "He had killed you, my Lord Antonio, had we not come."

But Antonio pointed to the body of Venusta. And she, at the instant, moaned again, and turned on her back, and gasped, and died: yet just before she died, her eyes sought Antonio's eyes, and he dropped suddenly on his knees beside her, and took her hand and kissed her brow. And they saw that she smiled in dying.

Then Lorenzo brushed a hand across his eyes and said to Antonio, "Suffer me to go back with my men, and for a week there shall be a truce between us."

"Let it be so," said Antonio.

And Bena smiled, for he knew that the Lieutenant of the Guard must now be near at hand. But this he did not tell Antonio, fearing that Antonio would tell Lorenzo. Then Lorenzo, with uncovered head, passed through the rank of Tommasino's men; and he took up his dead, and with them went down the path, leaving Venusta where she lay. And when he had gone two miles, he met the Lieutenant and his party, pressing on. Yet when the two companies had joined, they were no more than seventeen whole and sound men, so many of Lorenzo's had Tommasino's party slain or hurt. Therefore Lorenzo in his heart was not much grieved at the truce, for it had been hard with seventeen to force the path to the cave against ten, all unhurt and sound. And, having sorely chidden the Lieutenant of the Guard, he rode back, and rested that night in Venusta's house at Rilano, and the next day rode on to Firmola, and told Duke Valentine how the expedition had sped.

Then said Duke Valentine, "Force I have tried, and guile I have tried, and yet this man is delivered from my hand. Fortune fights for him;" and in chagrin and displeasure he went into his cabinet, and spoke to no man, and showed himself nowhere in the city, for the space of three days. But the townsmen, though they dared make no display, rejoiced that Antonio was safe, and the more because the Duke had laid so cunning and treacherous a snare for him.

Now Antonio, Tommasino, and the rest, when they were left alone, stood round the corpse of Venusta, and Antonio told them briefly all the story of her treachery as she herself had told it to him.

And when he had finished the tale, Bena cried, "She has deserved her death."

But Tommasino stooped down and composed her limbs and her raiment gently with his hand, and when he rose up his eyes were dim, and he said, "Yes; but at the last she gave her life for Antonio. And though she deserved death, it grieves me that she is gone to her account thus, without confession, pardon, or the rites of Holy Church.

Then Antonio said, "Behold, her death is her confession, and the same should be her pardon. And for the rites——"

He bent over her, and he dipped the tip of his finger in the lady's blood that had flowed from her wounded breast; and lightly with his finger-tip he signed the Cross in her own blood on her brow. "That," said he, "shall be her Unction; and I think, Tommasino, it will serve."

Thus the Lady Venusta died, and they carried her body down to Rilano and buried it there. And in after-days a tomb was raised over her, which may still be seen. But Count Antonio, being rejoined by such of his company as had escaped by flight from the pursuit of the Duke's troop, abode still in the hills, and albeit that his force was less, yet by the dread of his name and of the deeds that he had done he still defied the power of the Duke, and was not brought to submission.

And whether the poor youth whom Luigi pushed over the precipice lived or died, Niccolo knew not. But Luigi, having entered the service of the Duke, played false to him also, and, being convicted on sure evidence of taking to himself certain moneys that the Duke had charged him to distribute to the poor, was hanged in the great square a year to the very day after Venusta died; whereat let him grieve who will; I grieve not.

CHAPTER VIII.

THE MANNER OF COUNT ANTONIO'S RETURN.

In all that I have written concerning Count Antonio, I have striven to say that only which is surely based on truth and attested by credible witness, and have left on one side the more marvellous tales such as the credulity of ignorance and the fond licence of legend are wont to weave. But as to the manner of his return there is no room for uncertainty, for the whole account of it was recorded in the archives of the city by order of Duke Valentine the Good, son and successor to that Duke who outlawed Antonio; to which archives I, Ambrose, have had full access; and I have now free permission to make known so much of them as may serve for the proper understanding of the matter. And this same task is one to which I set my pen willingly, conceiving that the story is worthy of being known to every man in the Duchy; for while many may censure the things that Antonio did in the days of his sojourn in the hills, there can, I think, be none that will not look with approval on his bearing in this last hap of fortune. Indeed he was a gallant gentleman; and if, for that, I forgive him his sins too readily, in like manner may our good St. Prisian intercede that my sins be forgiven me.

Five years had the Count dwelt in the hills; five years had the Lady Lucia mourned in the city; five years had Duke Valentine laid plans and schemes. Then it fell out that a sickness came upon the city and the country round it; many died, and more were sore stricken but by the mercy of God narrowly escaped. Among those that suffered were the Duke himself, and at the same time a certain gentleman, by name Count Philip of Garda, a friend of Antonio's, and yet an obedient servant to the Duke. Now when Antonio heard that Philip lay sick, he sent to him a rich gift of choice meats and fruits by the hand of Tommasino. And Tommasino came with six of the band and delivered the gift, and might have ridden back in all safety, as did the six who came with him. But Philip had a fair daughter, and Tommasino, caught by her charms, made bold to linger at Philip's house, trusting that his presence there would not be known to the Duke, and venturing his own neck for the smiles of red lips and the glances of bright eyes, as young men have since this old world began. But one of the Duke's spies, of whom he maintained many, brought word to him of Tommasino's rashness; and as Tommasino at last rode forth privily in the evening, singing a love-song and hugging in his bosom a glove that the lady had suffered him to carry off, he came suddenly into an ambush of the Duke's Guard, was pulled violently from his horse, and before he could so much as draw his sword, behold, his arms were seized, and the Lord Lorenzo stood before him, with doffed cap and mocking smile!

"My glove is like to cost me dear," said Tommasino.

"Indeed, my lord," answered Lorenzo, "I fear

there will be a reckoning for it." Then he gave the word, and they set Tommasino bound on his horse, and rode without drawing rein to the city. And when the Duke heard the next morning of Tommasino's capture, he raised himself on his couch, where he lay in the shade by the fish-pond under the wall of his garden. "This is sweet medicine for my sickness," said he. "On the third day from now, at noon, he shall die. Bid them raise a great gibbet in front of my palace, so high that it shall be seen from every part of the city and from beyond the walls; and on that gibbet Tommasino shall hang, that all men may know that I, Valentine, am Duke and Lord of Firmola." And he lay back again, pale and faint.

But when word came to Antonio that Tommasino was taken, he withdrew himself from the rest of the band who were lamenting the untoward chance, and walked by himself to and fro for a long while. And he gazed once on the picture of the Lady Lucia which was always round his neck. Then he sat down and wrote a letter to the Duke, saying, " My gracious lord,

I am here with fifty men, stout and brave fellows; and if my cousin dies, there shall be no peace in the Duchy. But my heart is heavy already for those that have died in my quarrel, and I may not endure Tommasino's death. Therefore let Tommasino go, and grant full pardon and oblivion to him and to all who are here with me, and swear to do this with a binding oath; and then I will come and deliver myself to you, and suffer such doom as seems good to Your Highness. May Almighty God assuage Your Highness's sickness and keep you in all things.—Antonio of Monte Velluto." And this letter he sent to the Duke Valentine, who, having received it, pondered long, but at last said to Lorenzo, "I do not love to let Tommasino go, nor to pardon these lawless knaves; yet for five years I have pursued Antonio and have not taken him. And I am weary, and the country is racked and troubled by our strife."

"With Antonio dead, all would be quiet, my lord," said Lorenzo.

Then the Duke's eyes flashed and he said, "It shall be so. And bid them strengthen the gibbet, for Antonio is a large man; and he shall surely hang on it."

Now Lorenzo was somewhat grieved, for he esteemed Antonio; yet he obeyed the Duke's commands, and took from the Duke a letter for Antonio, wherein His Highness swore to all that Antonio asked, and bade him come alone or with one companion only into the city on the day that had been before appointed for the hanging of Tommasino. And, further, the Lord Lorenzo gathered together all the pikemen and every man that served the Duke, and placed them all on guard, and proclaimed that any man besides found carrying arms in the city should be held as the Duke's enemy. For he feared that the townsmen who loved Antonio would attempt something on his behalf. But when the townsmen saw the great force that Lorenzo had gathered, they dared attempt nothing, although they were sore grieved and lamented bitterly. And the Lady Lucia, looking from the window of her house, beheld those who were erecting the gibbet, and wept for her lover. As for Tommasino, when he heard that he was not to be hanged, but to be set free, and Antonio to suffer death in his stead, he was like a man mad, and his rage and grief could not be restrained; for he declared that he would not live if Antonio died, and did not cease to reproach himself bitterly. Therefore the Lord Lorenzo held him confined in his own house, lest he should do himself some harm, or endeavour by some desperate device to prevent Antonio from fulfilling his purpose; but he treated him with all courtesy, for he was sorry for his plight.

Now Count Antonio feared his companions and did not dare to tell them of what he had done, lest their obedience should fail under a strain so great, and they should by force prevent his going to the city. Therefore he told them to rest quiet in their camp, while he, with Bena, went about certain necessary business; and he bade them farewell, enjoining them most strictly to do nothing against the Duke.

"For," said he, "although I may not tell you fully what the business is on which I go, yet I have good hope that His Highness is favourably inclined to you, and that in a short space you will receive from him pardon for all your offences. And that pardon I charge you to accept with gratitude, and, having accepted it, be thenceforward loyal servants to His Highness."

"But will the Duke pardon you also, my lord, and the Lord Tommasino?" asked Martolo.

"He will pardon Tommasino also," answered Antonio. "And be assured that I shall suffer nothing." And having said this, he shook every man by the hand, thanking them for the love and service they had shown him; and he and Bena were accompanied by all of them to the foot of Mount Agnino; and there, in the early morning of the appointed day, Antonio mounted his horse and rode with Bena into the plain. And as they rode, Bena said to him, "My lord, why does the Duke grant this pardon?"

"Because I give him what he asks as the price of it, Bena," answered Antonio; and they rode on for a while. But when Bena saw that Antonio turned his horse not towards Rilano, but directly across the plain towards Firmola, he said, "My lord, whither are we riding?"

"We are riding to the city, Bena," answered Antonio. "There is no cause for fear; we go by leave and on the invitation of His Highness."

"But will he let us go again?" asked Bena.

"You will be free to go when you will," answered Antonio, "and me the Duke will himself send forth from the city when I am ready to go." For Lorenzo had promised in the Duke's name that Antonio's body, after it had hung three days on the gibbet, should be carried from the city to the church of St. Prisian at Rilano, and there interred with fitting ceremony.

"Yet I do not like this ride of ours," grumbled Bena.

"Nay, I like it not myself," said Antonio, smiling. "But for the good of my cousin and of all our company, we must go forward." And he stopped for a moment and added, "Swear to me, Bena, by St. Prisian, to obey in all I bid you in the city to-day, and not to draw your sword unless I draw mine."

"Do I not always obey you, my lord?" asked Bena.

"But swear to me."

"Well, then, I swear," said Bena, "though in truth, my lord, your word is full as strong to me as any oath, whether by Prisian or another." For this man whom they called Bena was a godless man, and one that held holy things in light esteem. But he was a fine fighter and a loyal servant, and God's mercy is infinite. It may be his heart was turned at last; though indeed I have found no record of it.

"My lord, will you see my Lady Lucia in the city?" asked Bena.

"I trust at the least to see her face at her window," answered Antonio.

"Will you have speech with her, my lord?"

"If His Highness will grant me that favour, Bena."

"Ah, I know now why you smiled, my lord, as you rode, just now. It will be a bright day for you." And Bena laughed.

"Indeed," said Antonio, "I trust that the day may be bright for me. Yes, bright as the light of heaven."

"There is no light brighter than the eyes of the girl a man loves," said Bena.

"Yes, there is one," said Antonio. But Bena did not understand his meaning.

Thus they rode till it wanted only two hours of noon; and then they were within five miles of the city, and Bena, looking, beheld the great gibbet rising above the walls of the city and standing forth grim and black in front of the marble face of the Cathedral.

"What is that, my lord," he cried, "which towers above the walls of the city?"

"Is it not enough to know when we come there?" answered Antonio.

Then Bena sighed, and said to Antonio, "I find it in my heart, my lord, to be half sorry that the Duke pardons us; for we lived a fine merry life in the hills. Yet it will be pleasant to live at ease: and we have adventures enough to tell our sweethearts, aye, and our children too, when we grow old, and they come round us and ask us for stories of our youth. I hope my boys will be good at a fight, my lord, and serve your sons as I have served you."

"It may be God's will that I leave no sons to bear my name, Bena."

"I do not think that," said Bena with a laugh.

They were now passing the hill on which stood the blackened walls of Antonio's house, which Duke Valentine had burnt.

Bena cried out at the sight. "You will need to spend much in rebuilding it," said he.

"Perhaps His Highness has provided another dwelling for me," said Antonio.

"To-night he will surely lodge you, my lord, in his own palace, or, may be, with my Lord Lorenzo."

"Wherever it may be, I shall sleep soundly," said Antonio.

Now they were come near to the city, and they saw a body of pikemen coming out to meet them, the Lieutenant of the Guard at the head. And when they met, the Lieutenant bowed to Antonio, who greeted him most courteously; and the pikemen spread themselves in front and behind and on both sides of Antonio and Bena, and thus they went on towards the bridge and the city gate. But Bena eyed the pikemen with no love, and moved restlessly in his saddle. "These fellows," said he to Antonio, "hem us in, my lord. Shall I make my horse threaten their toes a little, so that they may give us more room?"

"Let them be," said Antonio. "It is not for long, Bena."

At the entrance of the gate stood Lorenzo, awaiting the Count, and there they dismounted, and Antonio passed through the gate with Lorenzo, Bena being close to him on the other side. And when Bena saw the great force of pikemen, and, behind their ranks, a mighty throng of people, and when he saw the tall gibbet and understood what it was, suddenly his face went red and his hand flew to his sword.

But Antonio caught his arm, saying, "My sword is not drawn, Bena."

"My lord, what does it mean?" cried Bena in a loud voice, so that Lorenzo heard and stayed his steps and looked at Bena. "Does he not know?" he asked of Antonio.

"He does not know yet," said Antonio. And to Bena he said, "I have need of your sword, Bena. Give it me."

"My sword, my lord?"

"Yes, your sword."

Bena looked at him with wondering frightened eyes; but slowly he unbuckled his sword from his belt and gave it to Antonio. And Antonio unbuckled his own sword also and gave them both to the Lieutenant of the Guard, saying, "Sir, I pray you to restore Bena's to him in the evening, and mine to me when I go forth to Rilano."

But Bena clutched at Antonio's arm, crying again, "What does it mean, my lord?"

Then Antonio took him by the hand and said, "Are we to be afraid now of what we have often faced together with light hearts, Bena?"

"Are we to die?" asked Bena.

"You are to live and beget those brave boys, Bena. But it is otherwise with me," said Antonio.

Then the Lord Lorenzo, who had looked in Bena's eyes, signed to four pikemen to come near, and they came and stood near Bena; for Lorenzo feared that he would not suffer Antonio to die without seeking to save him or to die with him.

"Nay, let him alone," said Antonio. "You will obey me of your free-will, Bena?"

"Yes, my lord," said Bena; and he looked up at the gibbet; and then he caught Antonio's hand and kissed it a score of times; and he began to sob as a child sobs. And the Guard, among whom were some that had felt his arm, marvelled to see him thus moved.

"Let us go on," said Antonio. "It is hard on noon, and I must keep my tryst with His Highness."

His Highness awaits my lord by the fish-pond in the garden," said Lorenzo; and he led Antonio to the palace and brought him through the great hall and so to the fish-pond; and by it the Duke lay propped on pillows, yet very richly arrayed; and his little son sat by him. Now Lorenzo stood aloof, but Antonio came, and, kneeling, kissed the Duke's hand, and then rose and stood before the Duke. But the boy cried, "Why, it is my Lord Antonio! Have you come back to live in the city, my Lord Antonio? Ah, I am glad of it!"

"Nay, I have not come to live in the city, my little lord," said Antonio.

"Whither do you go then?" asked the boy.

"His Highness sends me on a journey," said Antonio.

"Is it far?"

"Yes, it is far," said Antonio with a smile.

"I wish he would send another and let you stay; then we could play at robbers again in the great hall," said the little Duke. "Father, can you find no other lord to go in Antonio's place?"

The Duke turned his face, pale and wasted with sickness, and his eyes, that seemed larger and deeper than they had been before, upon his son. "I can send none but Antonio," said he. And calling to Lorenzo, he bade him take the boy. But the boy went reluctantly, telling Antonio that he must return speedily. "For you promised," said he, "to teach me how to use my sword." And the Duke signed with his hand to Lorenzo, who lifted the boy and carried him away, leaving Antonio alone with the Duke.

"I have set my seal to the pardons as I swore," said the Duke; "and Tommasino shall be free this evening; and all that he and the rest have done against me shall be forgotten from this hour. Have you any cause of complaint against me?"

"None, my lord," said Count Antonio.

"Is there anything that you ask of me?"

"Nothing, my lord. Yet if it be Your Highness's pleasure that I should have speech with the Lady Lucia and with my cousin, I should be well pleased."

"You will see them yonder in the square," said the Duke. "But otherwise you shall not see them."

Then Lorenzo returned, and he led Antonio to a chamber and gave him meat and wine; and while Antonio ate, the Lord Archbishop, having heard that he was come, came in great haste; and the venerable man was very urgent with Antonio that he should make his peace with Heaven, so that, having confessed his sins and sought absolution, he might be relieved of the sentence of excommunication under which he lay, and be comforted with the rites of the Church before he died.

"For there are many wild and wicked deeds on your conscience," said the Archbishop, "and above all, the things that you did touching the Abbot of St. Prisian, and yet more impiously touching the Sacred Bones."

"Indeed I have many sins to confess," said Antonio; "but, my Lord Archbishop, concerning the Abbot and concerning the Sacred Bones I have nothing to confess. For even now, when I stand on the threshold of death, I can perceive nothing that I did save what I could not leave undone."

Then the Archbishop besought him very earnestly, and even with tears; but Antonio would own no sin in these matters, and therefore the Archbishop could not relieve him from his sentence nor give him the holy comforts, but left him and returned to his own house in great distress of spirit.

The Lord Lorenzo now came again to Antonio and said to him, "My lord, it wants but a few moments of noon." Therefore Antonio rose and went with him; and they came through the great hall, and, a strong escort being about them, took their stand at the foot of the palace steps. Then the Duke was borne out on his couch, high on the shoulders of his lackeys, and was set down on the topmost step: and silence having been proclaimed, the Duke spoke to Antonio; but so weak was his voice that none heard save those who were very near. "Antonio of Monte Velluto," said he, "it may be that in God's purposes I myself have not long to live. Yet it is long enough for me to uphold and vindicate that princely power which the same God has committed to my hands. That power you have outraged; many of my faithful friends you have slain; against both me and the Church you have lifted your hand. Go then to your death, that men may know the fate of traitors and of rebels."

Antonio bowed low to His Highness; but, not being invited by the Duke to speak, he said naught, but suffered Lorenzo to lead him across the square; and as he went, he passed where four pikemen stood by Bena, ready to lay hold on him if he moved; and Bena fell on his knees and again kissed Antonio's hand. And Antonio, passing on, saw two young lords, followers of Lorenzo. And between them stood Tommasino; their arms were through Tommasino's arms and they held him, though lovingly, yet firmly; and he had no sword.

"May I speak with Tommasino?" asked Antonio.

"His Highness has forbidden it," said Lorenzo; but Antonio paused for a moment before Tommasino; and Tommasino, greatly moved, cried piteously to him that he might die with him. And Antonio kissed him, and, with a shake of his head, passed on. Thus then he came to the gibbet, and mounted with Lorenzo on to the scaffold that was underneath the gibbet. And when he was seen there, a great groan went up from the people, and the apprenticed lads, who were all gathered together on the left side of the gibbet, murmured so fiercely and stirred so restlessly that the pikemen faced round, turning their backs towards the scaffold, and laid their pikes in rest.

Then the hour of noon struck from the clock in the tower of the Cathedral; and the Master of the Duke's Household, who stood by the couch of his master, turned his eyes to the Duke's face, seeking the signal for Antonio's death; which when he received, he would sign to the executioner to set the rope round the Count's neck; for the man stood by Antonio with the rope in his hand, and Antonio was already in his shirt. But when the Master of the Household looked at the Duke, the Duke made him no signal; yet the Duke had not fainted from his sickness, for he was propped on his elbow, his face was eager, and his gaze was set intently across the square; and his physician, who was near, spoke to him softly, saying, "My lord, they await the signal."

But the Duke waved him aside impatiently, and gazed still across the square. And, seeing His Highness thus gazing intently, the Master of the Household and the physician and all the rest who were about the Duke's person looked also; and they saw the Lady Lucia coming forth from her house, clad all in white. Antonio also saw her from where he stood on the scaffold, for the people made a way for her, and the pikemen let her pass through their ranks; so that she walked alone across the middle of the great square; and the eyes of all, leaving Antonio, were fixed upon her. Her face was very pale, and her hair fell on her shoulders; but she walked firmly and swiftly, and she turned neither to right nor left, but made straight for the spot where the Duke lay. And he, seeing her coming, moaned once, and passed his hand thrice across his eyes, and raised himself yet higher on his arm, leaning towards her over the side of the couch. Again he passed his hand across his brow; and the physician regarded him very intently, yet dared not again seek to rouse his attention, and imposed silence on the Master of the Household, who had asked in low tones, "What ails His Highness?" Then the Lady Lucia, having reached the foot of the steps, stood still there, her eyes on the Duke. Very fair was she, and sad, and she seemed rather some beautiful unsubstantial vision than a living maiden; and though she strove to form words with her lips, yet no words came; therefore it was by her muteness that she besought pity for herself and pardon for her lover. But the Duke, leaning yet further towards her, had fallen, but that the physician, kneeling, passed his arm round his body and held him up; and he said in low hoarse tones and like a man that is amazed and full of awe, and yet moved with a gladness so great that he cannot believe in it, "Who is it? Who is it?"

And the Lady Lucia still could not answer him. And he, craning towards her, spoke to her in entreaty, "Margherita, Margherita!"

Then indeed all marvelled; for the name that the Duke spoke was the name by which that Princess who had been his wife and was dead had been called; and they perceived that His Highness, overcome by his sickness, had lost discernment, and conceived the Lady Lucia to be not herself but the spirit of his dead love come to him from heaven, to which delusion her white robes and her death-like pallor might well incline him. And now the wonder and fear left his face, and there came in place of them a great joy and rapture, so that his sunk eyes gleamed, his lips quivered, and he beckoned with his hand, murmuring, "I am ready, I am ready, Margherita!" And while this passed, all who were too distant to hear the Duke's words wondered that the signal came not, but supposed that the Lady Lucia had interceded for Count Antonio, and that His Highness was now answering her prayer: and they hoped that he would grant it. And Antonio stood on the scaffold between the Lord Lorenzo and the executioner; and his eyes were set on Lucia.

Then the Duke spoke again to the Lady Lucia, saying, "I have been lonely, very lonely. How pale your face is, my sweet! Come to me. I cannot come to you, for I am very sick." And he held out his hand towards her again.

But she was now sore bewildered, for she could not understand the words which His Highness used to her, and she looked round, seeking some one who might tell her what they meant, but none moved from his place or came near to her; and at last she found voice enough to say in soft tones, "Antonio, my lord, the Count Antonio!"

"Aye, I know that you loved him," said the Duke. "But since then he has done great crimes, and he must die. Yet speak not of him now, but come here to me, Margherita."

Then, with wavering tread, she came towards him, mounting the first of the steps, and she said, "I know not what you would, my lord, nor why you call me by the name of Margherita. I am Lucia, and I come to ask Antonio's life."

"Lucia, Lucia?" said he, and his face grew doubtful. "Nay, but you are my Margherita," he said.

"No, my lord," she answered, as with trembling uncertain feet she mounted, till she stood but one step below where his couch was placed; and then she fell on her knees on the highest step and clasped her hands, crying, "Have mercy, my lord, have mercy! Think, my dear lord, how I love him; for if he dies, I must die also, my lord. Ah, my lord, you have known love. You loved our sweet Lady Margherita; was not her name now on your lips? So I love Antonio, so he loves me. Ah, my lord, Christ Jesus teaches pity!" And she buried her face in her hands and sobbed.

Then the Duke, his physician and now the Master of the Household also supporting him, stretched himself over the edge of his couch, and, putting out his hand with feverish strength, plucked the Lady Lucia's hands away from her face and gazed at her face. And when he had gazed a moment, he gave a great cry, "Ah, God!" and flung his arms up above his head and fell back into the arms of his physician, who laid him down on his couch, where he lay motionless, his eyes shut and his chin resting on his breast. And all looked at the physician, but he answered, "Nay, he is not dead yet."

"Why tarries the signal?" asked Antonio of Lorenzo on the scaffold.

"It must be that the Lady Lucia beseeches him for your life, my lord," answered Lorenzo. "Indeed heartily do I wish the Duke would hearken to her prayer."

"He will not turn for her," said Antonio.

But presently the report of what had passed spread from those round the Duke to the pikemen, and they, loving a marvel as most men do, must needs tell it to the people, and a murmur of wonder arose, and the report reached the guards at the scaffold, who came and told Lorenzo, in the hearing of Antonio, of the strange delusion that had come upon the Duke.

"He must be sick to death," said Lorenzo.

"I pray not," said Count Antonio. "For though he is a stern man, yet he is an able and just prince, and this fancy of his is very pitiful."

"Do you spare pity for him?" asked Lorenzo.

"Shall I not pity all who have lost their loves?" answered Antonio with a smile, and his eye rested on the form of the Lady Lucia kneeling by the Duke's couch.

For hard on half an hour the Duke lay as he had fallen, but at last, his physician having used all his skill to rouse him, he opened his eyes; and he clutched his physician's hand and pointed to Lucia, asking, "Who is she?"

"It is the Lady Lucia, my lord," answered the physician.

"And there was none else?" asked the Duke in a low tremulous whisper.

"I saw no other, my lord."

"But I saw her," said the Duke. "I saw her even as I saw her last, when she lay on her bed and they took the child out of her dead arms."

"It was the weakness of your malady, my lord, that made the vision before your eyes."

"Alas, was it no more?" moaned the Duke. "Indeed, I am very weak; there is a blur before my eyes. I cannot see who this lady is that kneels before me. Who is she, and what ails her?" And having said this in fretful weary tones, he lay back on his pillow gasping.

Then the Master of the Household came forward and said to him, "My lord, this is the Lady Lucia, and she kneels before your Highness praying for the life of Count Antonio, because she loves him."

Now the name of Count Antonio, when spoken to him, moved the Duke more than all the ministrations of his physician; he roused himself once again, crying, "Antonio! I had forgotten Antonio. Does he still live?"

"Your Highness has not given the signal for his death."

"Have I not? Then here——"

He moved his hand, but with a great cry the Lady Lucia sprang forward and seized his hand before he could raise it, kneeling to him and crying, "No, no, my lord, no, no, no!" And the Duke had no strength to fling her off, but he gasped, "Free me from her!" And the Master of the Household, terrified lest in her passion she should do violence to His Highness, roughly tore her hands from the Duke's hand, and the Duke, released, sat up on his couch, and he said, in a strange hard voice that was heard of all, even to the scaffold, and yet seemed not the voice that they knew as his, "Let Antonio——" But then he stopped; he choked in his throat, and, catching at his shirt, tore it loose from him. "Let Antonio!"——he cried again. "Let Antonio!"—— And he sat there for an instant; and his eyes grew dim, the intelligence departing from them; once again he opened his lips, but nothing came from them save a gasp; and with a thud he fell back on his pillows, and, having rolled once on his side, turned again on his back and lay still. And a great hush fell on every man in the square, and they looked in one another's faces, but found no answer.

For Valentine, Duke and Lord of Firmola, was dead of his sickness at the moment when he had sought to send Antonio to death. Thus marvellously did Heaven in its high purposes deal with him.

"His Highness is dead," said the physician. And the Master of the Household, as his duty was, came to the front of the Duke's couch, and, standing there before all the people, broke the wand of his office, and let the broken fragments fall upon the marble steps; and he cried aloud, "Hear all of you! It hath pleased Almighty God to take unto Himself the soul of the noble and illustrious Prince, Valentine, Duke and Lord of Firmola. May his soul find peace!"

But there came from the people no answering cry of "Amen," as, according to the custom of the Duchy, should have come. For they were amazed at the manner of this death; and many crossed themselves in fear, and women sobbed.

And Lorenzo, standing on the scaffold by Antonio, was struck with wonder and fear, and clutched Antonio's arm, crying, "Can it be that the Duke is dead?" And Antonio bowed his head, answering, "May Christ receive his soul!"

Then the Master of the Household came forward again and cried, "Hear all of you! According to the high pleasure and appointment of Almighty God, the noble and illustrious Prince, Valentine, Second of that Name, is from this hour Duke and Lord of Firmola; whom obey, serve, and honour, all of you. May his rule be prosperous!"

And this time there came a low murmur of "Amen" from the people. But before more could pass, there was a sudden commotion in the square before the scaffold. For Bena, seeing what was done, and knowing that the Duke was dead, had glanced at the pikemen who stood near; and when he saw that they looked not at him but towards where the Master of the Household stood, he sprang forward and ran like a deer to the scaffold; and he leapt up to the scaffold before any could hinder him, and he cried in a mighty loud voice, saying, "By what warrant do you hold my lord a prisoner?"

Then the apprentices raised a great cheer and with one accord pressed upon the pikemen, who, mazed by all that had passed, gave way before them; and the apprentices broke their bounds and surged like a billow of the sea up to the foot of the scaffold, shouting Antonio's name; and the young lords who held Tommasino came with him and broke through and reached the scaffold; for they feared for Lorenzo, and yet would not let Tommasino go: and Lorenzo was sore at a loss, but he drew his sword and cried that he would slay any man that touched Antonio, until the right of the matter should be known.

"Indeed, if you will give me a sword, I will slay him myself," said Antonio. "For I stand here by my own will, and according to the promise I gave to the Duke; and if there be lawful authority to hang me, hang me; but if not, dispose of me as the laws of the Duchy bid."

"I have no authority," said Lorenzo, "save what the Duke gave; and now he is dead."

Then the Count Antonio fastened his shirt again about his neck and put on his doublet; and he signed to Bena to stand on one side of him, and he bade the young lords loose Tommasino. And he said to Lorenzo, "Let us go together to the palace." And now he was smiling. Then they came down from the scaffold and passed across the square, a great multitude following them. And when they came to the steps of the palace, the Duke's body was covered with a rich brocaded cloth that some hand had brought from his cabinet; and the little Duke stood there with his hand in the Master of the Household's hand; and the child was weeping bitterly, for he was very frightened; and over against him stood the Lady Lucia, motionless as though she had been turned to stone; for the strange thing that had come about through her approaching of the Duke had bewildered her brain. But when the boy saw Antonio he let go the hand he held and ran to Antonio and leapt into his arms. Then Antonio lifted him and showed him to the people, who hailed him for Duke; and Antonio set him down and knelt before him and kissed his hand. And the child cried, "Now that my father is dead, Antonio, you must not go on your journey, but you must stay with me. For if I am Duke, I must learn to use my sword without delay, and no man but you shall teach me."

"Shall I not go on my journey, my lord?" asked Antonio.

"No, you shall not go," said the little Duke.

Then Antonio turned to the lords who stood round and said, "Behold, my lords, His Highness pardons me."

But the lords doubted; and they said to Antonio, "Nay, but he does not know what he does in pardoning you."

"He understands as well, I think," said Antonio, "as his father understood when he sent me to death. Indeed, my lords, it is not children only who know not what they do." And at this speech Tommasino smiled and Bena laughed gruffly. But the lords, bidding Antonio rest where he was till they returned, retired with the little Duke into the palace, and sent word hastily to the Archbishop that he should join them there and deliberate with them as to what it might be best to do. And when they were thus gone in, Antonio said, "I may not move, but the Lady Lucia is free to move."

Then Tommasino went to the lady and spoke to her softly, telling her that Antonio desired to speak with her; and she gave Tommasino her hand, and he led her to Antonio, who stood within the portico, screened from the sight of the people. And there they were left alone.

But meanwhile the whole body of the townsmen and the apprentices had gathered before the palace, and their one cry was for Antonio. For the fear of the Duke being no longer upon them, and the pikemen not knowing whom to obey and being therefore disordered, the people became very bold, and they had stormed the palace, had not one come to Antonio and implored him so show himself, that the people might know that he was safe. Therefore he came forward with the Lady Lucia, who was now no more bewildered, nor petrified with fear or astonishment, but was weeping with her eyes and smiling with her lips and clinging to Antonio's arm. And when the people saw them thus, they set up a great shout, that was heard far beyond the city walls; and the apprenticed lads turned and ran in a body across the square, and swarmed on to the scaffold. And then and there they plucked down the gibbet and worked so fiercely that in the space of half an hour there was none of it left.

And now the Archbishop with the lords came forth from the council chamber, and the little Duke with them. And they caused the servants to remove the body of the dead Duke, and they set his son on a high seat, and put a sceptre in his hand. And the Archbishop offered up a prayer before the people; and, having done this, he turned to Antonio and said, "My Lord Antonio, most anxiously have His Highness and we of his Council considered of this matter; and it has seemed to us all—my own in truth was the sole reluctant voice, and now I also am brought to the same mind—that whereas the virtuous purposes of princes are meet to be remembered and made perpetual by faithful fulfilment after their death, yet the errors of which they, being mortal, are guilty should not overlive them nor be suffered to endure when they have passed away. And though we are not blind to your offences, yet we judge that in the beginning the fault was not yours. Therefore His Highness decrees your pardon for all offences against his civil state and power. And I myself, who hold authority higher than any earthly might, seeing in what this day has witnessed the finger of God Himself, do not fight against it, but will pray you, so soon as you may fit yourself thereunto by prayer and meditation, to come in a humble mind and seek again the blessing of the Church. For in what you did right and in what you outstepped right, God Himself must one day judge, and I will seek to judge of it no more."

"My lord," said Antonio, "I have done much wrong. Yet I will own no wrong in the matter of the Abbot nor in that of the Sacred Bones."

But the lord Archbishop smiled at Antonio, and Antonio bent and kissed the ring that was on his finger; and the old man laid his hand for a moment on Antonio's head, saying, "It may be that God works sometimes in ways that I may not see."

Thus then it was that the Count Antonio was restored to his place, and came again to Firmola; and, having been relieved of the sentence of excommunication that had been laid upon him, he was wedded in the Cathedral to the Lady Lucia as soon as the days of mourning for the Duke had passed. And great was the joy in the city at their wedding; for every maid and every man saw in the triumph of Antonio's love a sign of the favour of Heaven to those who love with a pure and abiding passion. So they made great feasts, and were marvellously merry; and Bena let not the day go by without plighting his troth to a comely damsel, saying with a twinkle in his eye that the Count Antonio would have need of his sons, whose services he had promised to him as they rode together across the plain on the morning when Antonio had supposed that he was to die. Nor would Bena give any other reason whatsoever for the marriage. Nevertheless it is likely that there were others. But whether Bena fulfilled his promise I know not; for, as I have said, so little is known concerning him that his true name does not survive, and it has proved an impossible thing to discover whether any of his descendants yet live in Firmola. If it chance that they do, I trust that they fight as well, and serve as loyally, and pray better than he. But Martolo has left those that bear his name, and a great-grandson of his is at this very time huntsman to the Monastery of St. Prisian, where I have seen and talked with him many times.

The task which I laid upon myself thus finds its end. For there is no need for me to tell of the after-deeds of Count Antonio of Monte Velluto, nor how, in the space of a few months, he was chosen by all the lords to be Ruler and Protector of the State during the infancy of the Duke; in which high office he did many notable deeds, both of war and peace, and raised the Duchy to a great height of power, and conferred many favours on the townsmen of Firmola, whom he loved and cherished because they had not forsaken him nor ceased to love him during all the years that he dwelt an outlaw in the hills. And he built again his house on the hill which Duke Valentine had burnt, and dwelt there with Lucia, and with Tommasino also, until Tommasino took to wife that same lady for whose sake he had lingered and thus fallen into the hands of the lord Lorenzo, and went and dwelt at Rilano, where those of his house still dwell. But when the young Duke came of an age to reign, the Count Antonio delivered his charge into his hand, yet continued to counsel him, and was very high in authority. And neighbouring princes also sought his aid and his counsel, and he was greatly honoured of all men. Thus if there were aught in his youth that merits censure, it may be held that he blotted out the shame of it by his after-life, for his later days were filled with honourable service to his Prince and to his country.

Yet the heart of man is a vain thing; for when I, who am known to have learnt all that can be recovered from the mists of past times concerning Count Antonio, am asked—and whether it be by men or women, by boys or girls, aye, or by toddling infants—to tell them a tale of the great Count Antonio, it is not of the prudent ruler, nor of the wise counsellor, nay, nor even of the leader of the Duke's army, that they would hear, but always of Antonio when he was an outlaw, banned by his Prince and by the Church, living by the light of his own heart and by the strength of his own hand, secured only by the love and duty of the lawless men who followed him, and risking his life every day and every hour for the sake of the bright eyes of that lady who waited for him in the city. And when I, thinking to check this perversity, bid them look rather on his more worthy and sober days, they answer with a laugh, "But why, father, do you not write the story of those more worthy and sober days?" Nor will they believe when I say that it is but because the deeds of those days are elsewhere recorded. In good truth, I believe that in our hearts we love a lawless man! Here, then, ye perverse children, are the stories; they are all that you shall have from me. Read them; may they teach you to be true comrades, faithful lovers of one maid, and, since strife must needs come until God's pleasure bring peace to reign on earth, able, when occasion calls, to give and take good blows. Aye, never laugh. I have said it. A Churchman is a man.

THE END.

D. APPLETON & CO.'S PUBLICATIONS.

NOVELS BY HALL CAINE.

THE MANXMAN. 12mo. Cloth, $1.50.

"A story of marvelous dramatic intensity, and in its ethical meaning has a force comparable only to Hawthorne's 'Scarlet Letter.'"—*Boston Beacon.*

"A work of power which is another stone added to the foundation of enduring fame to which Mr. Caine is yearly adding."—*Public Opinion.*

"A wonderfully strong study of character; a powerful analysis of those elements which go to make up the strength and weakness of a man, which are at fierce warfare within the same breast; contending against each other, as it were, the one to raise him to fame and power, the other to drag him down to degradation and shame. Never in the whole range of literature have we seen the struggle between these forces for supremacy over the man more powerfully, more realistically delineated than Mr. Caine pictures it."—*Boston Home Journal.*

THE DEEMSTER. A Romance of the Isle of Man. 12mo. Cloth, $1.50.

"Hall Caine has already given us some very strong and fine work, and 'The Deemster' is a story of unusual power. . . . Certain passages and chapters have an intensely dramatic grasp, and hold the fascinated reader with a force rarely excited nowadays in literature."—*The Critic.*

"One of the strongest novels which has appeared in many a day."—*San Francisco Chronicle.*

"Fascinates the mind like the gathering and bursting of a storm."—*Illustrated London News.*

"Deserves to be ranked among the remarkable novels of the day."—*Chicago Times.*

THE BONDMAN. New edition. 12mo. Cloth, $1.50.

"The welcome given to this story has cheered and touched me, but I am conscious that, to win a reception so warm, such a book must have had readers who brought to it as much as they took away. . . . I have called my story a saga, merely because it follows the epic method, and I must not claim for it at any point the weighty responsibility of history, or serious obligations to the world of fact. But it matters not to me what Icelanders may call 'The Bondman,' if they will honor me by reading it in the open hearted spirit and with the free mind with which they are content to read of Grettir and of his fights with the Troll."—*From the Author's Preface.*

CAPT'N DAVY'S HONEYMOON. A Manx Yarn. 12mo. Paper, 50 cents; cloth, $1.00.

"A new departure by this author. Unlike his previous works, this little tale is almost wholly humorous, with, however, a current of pathos underneath. It is not always that an author can succeed equally well in tragedy and in comedy, but it looks as though Mr. Hall Caine would be one of the exceptions."—*London Literary World.*

"It is pleasant to meet the author of 'The Deemster' in a brightly humorous little story like this. . . . It shows the same observation of Manx character, and much of the same artistic skill."—*Philadelphia Times.*

New York: D. APPLETON & CO., 72 Fifth Avenue.

D. APPLETON & CO.'S PUBLICATIONS.

By A. CONAN DOYLE.

THE STARK MUNRO LETTERS. Being a Series of Twelve Letters written by J. STARK MUNRO, M. B., to his friend and former fellow-student, Herbert Swanborough, of Lowell, Massachusetts, during the years 1881-1884. Illustrated. 12mo. Buckram, $1.50.

This original and dramatic story presents fresh types, extraordinary situations, and novel suggestions with a freshness and vigor which show that the romancer's heart was in his work. How far certain incidents of the story are based upon personal experiences it is impossible to say, but the unflagging interest and unexpected phases of the romance are no less in evidence than the close personal relations established between author and reader. In the "Stark Munro Letters" the author has achieved another success which will add to the number of his American friends and readers.

"Any one who has read any of the fascinating stories in which the shrewd detective, Sherlock Holmes, figures as the very personification of detective logic applied to the detection of crime, knows that Conan Doyle is a story-teller of the very first order of merit. Like his own character, Sherlock Holmes, he possesses the power of getting out of everything all there is in it."—*Philadelphia Item.*

"Dr. Doyle's stories are so well known for their strong dramatic style, for the elegance of expression, that anything new from his pen is sure to be warmly welcomed. His readers are sure of getting a literary treat from anything he writes. He is broadminded and liberal, and the man who could write two such books as 'The White Company' and 'The Refugees' has a future which the shades of Scott and Dickens might envy."—*Albany Times-Union.*

SEVENTH EDITION.

ROUND THE RED LAMP. 12mo. Cloth, $1.50.

The "Red Lamp," the trade-mark, as it were, of the English country practitioner's office, is the central point of these dramatic stories of professional life. There are no secrets for the surgeon, and, a surgeon himself as well as a novelist, the author has made a most artistic use of the motives and springs of action revealed to him in a field of which he is the master.

"Too much can not be said in praise of these strong productions, that, to read, keep one's heart leaping to the throat and the mind in a tumult of anticipation to the end. . . . No series of short stories in modern literature can approach them."—*Hartford Times.*

"If Mr. A. Conan Doyle had not already placed himself in the front rank of living English writers by 'The Refugees,' and other of his larger stories, he would surely do so by these fifteen short tales."—*New York Mail and Express.*

"The reading of these choice stories will prove an exciting pleasure to all who may linger on the pages that present them."—*Boston Courier.*

"A strikingly realistic and decidedly original contribution to modern literature."—*Boston Saturday Evening Gazette.*

"Every page reveals the literary artist, the keen observer, the trained delineator of human nature, its weal and its woe. . . . Dr. Doyle has a rich note-book or, we should say, a golden memory."—*London Freeman's Journal.*

New York: D. APPLETON & CO., 72 Fifth Avenue.

D. APPLETON & CO.'S PUBLICATIONS.

S. R. CROCKETT'S LATEST BOOKS.

UNIFORM EDITION. EACH, 12MO. CLOTH, $1.50.

BOG-MYRTLE AND PEAT.

"Here are idyls, epics, dramas of human life, written in words that thrill and burn.... Each is a poem that has an immortal flavor. They are fragments of the author's early dreams, too bright, too gorgeous, too full of the blood of rubies and the life of diamonds to be caught and held palpitating in expression's grasp."—*Boston Courier.*

"Contains some of the most dramatic pieces Mr. Crockett has yet written, and in these picturesque sketches he is altogether delightful.... The volume is well worth reading—all of it."—*Philadelphia Press.*

"Hardly a sketch among them all that will not afford pleasure to the reader for its genial humor, artistic local coloring, and admirable portrayal of character."—*Boston Home Journal.*

"One dips into the book anywhere and reads on and on, fascinated by the writer's charm of manner."—*Minneapolis Tribune.*

"These stories are lively and vigorous, and have many touches of human nature in them—such touches as we are used to from having read 'The Stickit Minister' and 'The Lilac Sunbonnet.'"—*New Haven Register.*

"'Bog-Myrtle and Peat' contains stories which could only have been written by a man of genius."—*London Chronicle.*

THE LILAC SUNBONNET. A Love Story.

"A love story pure and simple, one of the old-fashioned, wholesome, sunshiny kind, with a pure-minded, sound-hearted hero, and a heroine who is merely a good and beautiful woman; and if any other love story half so sweet has been written this year, it has escaped our notice."—*New York Times.*

"A solid novel with an old time flavor, as refreshing when compared to the average modern story as is a whiff of air from the hills to one just come from a hothouse."—*Boston Beacon.*

"The general conception of the story, the motive of which is the growth of love between the young chief and heroine, is delineated with a sweetness and a freshness, a naturalness and a certainty, which places 'The Lilac Sunbonnet' among the best stories of the time."—*New York Mail and Express.*

"In its own line this little love story can hardly be excelled. It is a pastoral, an idyl—the story of love and courtship and marriage of a fine young man and a lovely girl—no more. But it is told in so thoroughly delightful a manner, with such playful humor, such delicate fancy, such true and sympathetic feeling, that nothing more could be desired."—*Boston Traveller.*

"A charming love story, redolent of the banks and braes and lochs and pines, healthy to the core, the love that God made for man and woman's first glimpse of paradise, and a constant reminder of it."—*San Francisco Call.*

New York: D. APPLETON & CO., 72 Fifth Avenue.

D. APPLETON & CO.'S PUBLICATIONS.

THE RED BADGE OF COURAGE. A Tale of the Civil War. By STEPHEN CRANE. 12mo. Cloth, $1.00.

"For an equally searching and graphic analysis of the volunteer in battle, one is tempted to turn to certain pages of Tolstoy. Mr. Crane puts before us the reality of war as it appeared to the soldier, and the interest of his picture is intense and absorbing."

A STREET IN SUBURBIA. By EDWIN PUGH. 12mo. Cloth, $1.00.

"Simplicity of style, strength, and delicacy of character study will mark this book as one of the most significant of the year."—*New York Press.*

"Thoroughly entertaining, and more—it shows traces of a creative genius something akin to Dickens."—*Boston Traveller.*

"In many respects the best of all the books of lighter literature brought out this season."—*Providence News.*

MAJESTY. A Novel. By LOUIS COUPERUS. Translated by A. TEIXEIRA DE MATTOS and ERNEST DOWSON. 12mo. Cloth, $1.00.

"No novelist whom we can call to mind has ever given the world such a masterpiece of royal portraiture as Louis Couperus's striking romance entitled 'Majesty.'"—*Philadelphia Record.*

"There is not an uninteresting page in the book, and it ought to be read by all who desire to keep in line with the best that is published in modern fiction."—*Buffalo Commercial.*

THE NEW MOON. By C. E. RAIMOND, author of "George Mandeville's Husband," etc. 12mo. Cloth, $1.00.

"A delicate pathos makes itself felt as the narrative progresses, whose cadences fall on the spirit's consciousness with a sweet and soothing influence not to be measured in words."—*Boston Courier.*

"One of the most impressive of recent works of fiction, both for its matter and especially for its presentation."—*Milwaukee Journal.*

THE WISH. A Novel. By HERMANN SUDERMANN. With a Biographical Introduction by ELIZABETH LEE. 12mo. Cloth, $1.00.

"Contains some superb specimens of original thought."—*New York World.*

"The style is direct and incisive, and holds the unflagging attention of the reader."—*Boston Journal.*

"A powerful story, very simple, very direct."—*Chicago Evening Post.*

New York: D. APPLETON & CO., 72 Fifth Avenue.

D. APPLETON & CO.'S PUBLICATIONS.

STONEPASTURES. By ELEANOR STUART. 16mo. Cloth, 75 cents.

This graphic picture of quaint characters belongs to the class of specialized American fiction which has been headed by the work of Miss Wilkins, Mr. Cable, Colonel Johnston, Mr. Garland, and others. The author has studied the peculiar and almost unknown life of the laborers in a Pennsylvania mining and manufacturing town with a keenness of observation and an abundant sense of humor which will give her book a permanent place among the *genre* studies of American life.

THE WATTER'S MOU'. By BRAM STOKER. 16mo. Cloth, 75 cents.

"Told with directness and power, and is an exceptionally strong piece of work."—*Boston Journal.*

"The characters are strongly drawn, the descriptions are intensely dramatic, and the situations are portrayed with rare vividness of language. It is a thrilling story, told with great power."—*Boston Advertiser.*

MASTER AND MAN. By Count LEO TOLSTOY. With an Introduction by W. D. HOWELLS. 16mo. Cloth, 75 cents.

"Crowded with these characteristic touches which mark his literary work."—*Public Opinion.*

"From the very start the reader feels that it is from a master's pen."—*Boston Times.*

"Reveals a wonderful knowledge of the workings of the human mind, and it tells a tale that not only stirs the emotions, but gives us a better insight into our own hearts."—*San Francisco Argonaut.*

THE ZEIT-GEIST. By L. DOUGALL, author of "The Mermaid," "Beggars All," etc. 16mo. Cloth, 75 cents.

"It is impossible for one to read it without feeling better for having done so—without having a desire to aid his fellow-men."—*New York Times.*

"One of the best of the short stories of the day."—*Boston Journal.*

"One of the most remarkable novels of the year."—*New York Commercial Advertiser.*

"Powerful in conception, treatment, and influence."—*Boston Globe.*

THE GREEN CARNATION. 12mo. Buckram, 75 cents.

"Here are wit and badinage that cut like two-edged rapiers; here is the true Gallic salt well rubbed into the raw places on the sleek body of the Philistine; here is the mirror held up to a false respectability; and all the while the epigrams tread close upon one another's heels in bewildering brilliancy."—*Philadelphia Evening Bulletin.*

New York: D. APPLETON & CO., 72 Fifth Avenue.

D. APPLETON & CO.'S PUBLICATIONS.

CORRUPTION. By PERCY WHITE, author of "Mr. Bailey-Martin," etc. 12mo. Cloth, $1.25.

The promise shown in "Mr. Bailey-Martin" reaches fulfillment in this acute study of political and social adventures in London. The story illustrates phases of life which are of especial interest, and it is told with rare felicity of expression by an author intimately acquainted with the subjects of which he treats.

A HARD WOMAN. A Story in Scenes. By VIOLET HUNT. 12mo. Cloth, $1.25.

This brilliant picture of certain types and phases of modern London life will be read and talked about for its originality and power. The author has varied the usual form of fiction, and her study of artistic and fashionable society will be found intensely modern in spirit, bright and entertaining throughout.

AN IMAGINATIVE MAN. By ROBERT S. HICHENS, author of "The Green Carnation." 12mo. Cloth, $1.25.

"One of the brightest books of the year."—*Boston Budget*.

"Altogether delightful, fascinating, unusual."—*Cleveland Amusement Gazette*.

"A study in character. . . . Just as entertaining as though it were the conventional story of love and marriage. The clever hand of the author of 'The Green Carnation' is easily detected in the caustic wit and pointed epigram."—*Jeannette L. Gilder, in the New York World*.

IN THE FIRE OF THE FORGE. A Romance of Old Nuremberg. By GEORG EBERS, author of "Cleopatra," "An Egyptian Princess," etc. In 2 vols. 16mo. Paper, 80 cents; cloth, $1.50.

"The tale is vividly told in language whose vigorous style is beautified by genuine poetic grace. Whatever Dr. Ebers writes is bound to interest and instruct—rea on sufficient why his books should be chosen in place of the emotional trash that too often appeals to the average mind."—*Boston Budget*.

THE LAND OF THE SUN. *Vistas Mexicanas.* By CHRISTIAN REID, author of "The Land of the Sky," "A Comedy of Elopement," etc. Illustrated. 12mo. Cloth, $1.75.

"Perhaps no book of recent date gives a simpler and at the same time more effective picture of this truly beautiful 'land of the sun' than is to be found in this striking volume."—*St. Louis Republic*.

"One of the most charming books of travel that we have read for a long time. . . . Certainly no one should ever think of visiting Mexico without taking this book of splendid description and delightful romance with him."—*Boston Home Journal*.

"He who would see the grandeurs of Mexico through the eyes of another should give careful perusal to Christian Reid's portrayal of 'The Land of the Sun,' which in every detail is a fitting tribute to the past, present, and future conditions of the new Spain."—*Chicago Evening Post*.

New York: D. APPLETON & CO., 72 Fifth Avenue.

D. APPLETON & CO.'S PUBLICATIONS.

NOVELS BY MAARTEN MAARTENS.

THE GREATER GLORY. *A Story of High Life.* By MAARTEN MAARTENS, author of "God's Fool," "Joost Avelingh," etc. 12mo. Cloth, $1.50.

"Until the Appletons discovered the merits of Maarten Maartens, the foremost of Dutch novelists, it is doubtful if many American readers knew that there were Dutch novelists. His 'God's Fool' and 'Joost Avelingh' made for him an American reputation. To our mind this just published work of his is his best. . . . He is a master of epigram, an artist in description, a prophet in insight."—*Boston Advertiser.*

"It would take several columns to give any adequate idea of the superb way in which the Dutch novelist has developed his theme and wrought out one of the most impressive stories of the period. . . . It belongs to the small class of novels which one can not afford to neglect."—*San Francisco Chronicle.*

"Maarten Maartens stands head and shoulders above the average novelist of the day in intellectual subtlety and imaginative power."—*Boston Beacon.*

GOD'S FOOL. By MAARTEN MAARTENS. 12mo. Cloth, $1.50.

"Throughout there is an epigrammatic force which would make palatable a less interesting story of human lives or one less deftly told."—*London Saturday Review.*

"Perfectly easy, graceful, humorous. . . . The author's skill in character-drawing is undeniable."—*London Chronicle.*

"A remarkable work."—*New York Times.*

"Maarten Maartens has secured a firm footing in the eddies of current literature. . . . Pathos deepens into tragedy in the thrilling story of 'God's Fool.'"—*Philadelphia Ledger.*

"Its preface alone stamps the author as one of the leading English novelists of to-day."—*Boston Daily Advertiser.*

"The story is wonderfully brilliant. . . . The interest never lags; the style is realistic and intense; and there is a constantly underlying current of subtle humor. . . . It is, in short, a book which no student of modern literature should fail to read."—*Boston Times.*

"A story of remarkable interest and point."—*New York Observer.*

JOOST AVELINGH. By MAARTEN MAARTENS. 12mo. Cloth, $1.50.

"So unmistakably good as to induce the hope that an acquaintance with the Dutch literature of fiction may soon become more general among us."—*London Morning Post.*

"In scarcely any of the sensational novels of the day will the reader find more, nature or more human nature."—*London Standard.*

"A novel of a very high type. At once strongly realistic and powerfully idealistic."—*London Literary World.*

"Full of local color and rich in quaint phraseology and suggestion."—*London Telegraph.*

"Maarten Maartens is a capital story-teller."—*Pall Mall Gazette.*

"Our English writers of fiction will have to look to their laurels."—*Birmingham Daily Post.*

New York: D. APPLETON & CO., 72 Fifth Avenue.

D. APPLETON & CO.'S PUBLICATIONS.

MANY INVENTIONS. By RUDYARD KIPLING. Containing fourteen stories, several of which are now published for the first time, and two poems. 12mo, 427 pages. Cloth, $1.50.

"The reader turns from its pages with the conviction that the author has no superior to-day in animated narrative and virility of style. He remains master of a power which none of his contemporaries approach him—the ability to select out of countless details the few vital ones which create the finished picture. He knows how, with a phrase or a word, to make you see his characters as he sees them, to make you feel the full meaning of a dramatic situation."—*New York Tribune.*

"'Many Inventions' will confirm Mr. Kipling's reputation. . . . We would cite with pleasure sentences from almost every page, and extract incidents from almost every story. But to what end? Here is the completest book that Mr. Kipling has yet given us in workmanship, the weightiest and most humane in breadth of view."—*Pall Mall Gazette.*

"Mr. Kipling's powers as a story-teller are evidently not diminishing. We advise everybody to buy 'Many Inventions,' and to profit by some of the best entertainment that modern fiction has to offer."—*New York Sun.*

"'Many Inventions' will be welcomed wherever the English language is spoken. . . . Every one of the stories bears the imprint of a master who conjures up incident as if by magic, and who portrays character, scenery, and feeling with an ease which is only exceeded by the boldness of force."—*Boston Globe.*

"The book will get and hold the closest attention of the reader."—*American Bookseller.*

"Mr. Rudyard Kipling's place in the world of letters is unique. He sits quite aloof and alone, the incomparable and inimitable master of the exquisitely fine art of short-story writing. Mr. Robert Louis Stevenson has perhaps written several tales which match the run of Mr. Kipling's work, but the best of Mr. Kipling's tales are matchless, and his latest collection, 'Many Inventions,' contains several such."—*Philadelphia Press.*

"Of late essays in fiction the work of Kipling can be compared to only three—Blackmore's 'Lorna Doone,' Stevenson's marvelous sketch of Villon in the 'New Arabian Nights,' and Thomas Hardy's 'Tess of the D'Urbervilles.' . . . It is probably owing to this extreme care that 'Many Inventions' is undoubtedly Mr. Kipling's best book."—*Chicago Post.*

"Mr. Kipling's style is too well known to American readers to require introduction, but it can scarcely be amiss to say there is not a story in this collection that does not more than repay a perusal of them all."—*Baltimore American.*

"As a writer of short stories Rudyard Kipling is a genius. He has had imitators, but they have not been successful in dimming the luster of his achievements by contrast. . . . 'Many Inventions' is the title. And they are inventions—entirely original in incident, ingenious in plot, and startling by their boldness and force."—*Rochester Herald.*

"How clever he is! This must always be the first thought on reading such a collection of Kipling's stories. Here is art—art of the most consummate sort. Compared with this, the stories of our brightest young writers become commonplace."—*New York Evangelist.*

"Taking the group as a whole, it may be said that the execution is up to his best in the past, while two or three sketches surpass in rounded strength and vividness of imagination anything else he has done."—*Hartford Courant.*

"Fifteen more extraordinary sketches, without a tinge of sensationalism, it would be hard to find. . . . Every one has an individuality of its own which fascinates the reader."—*Boston Times.*

D. APPLETON & CO., 72 Fifth Avenue, New York.

D. APPLETON & CO.'S PUBLICATIONS.

GILBERT PARKER'S BEST BOOKS.

"Mr. Parker has been named more than once, and in quarters of repute, 'the coming man.'"—LONDON LITERARY WORLD.

The Trail of the Sword.

Paper, 50 cents; cloth, $1.00.

Philadelphia Bulletin.

"Mr. Parker here adds to a reputation already wide, and anew demonstrates his power of pictorial portrayal and of strong dramatic situation and climax."

Pittsburg Times.

"The tale holds the reader's interest from first to last, for it is full of fire and spirit, abounding in incident, and marked by good character drawing."

The Trespasser.

Paper, 50 cents; cloth, $1.00.

The Critic.

"Interest, pith, force, and charm—Mr. Parker's new story possesses all these qualities. . . . Almost bare of synthetical decoration, his paragraphs are stirring because they are real. We read at times—as we have read the great masters of romance—breathlessly."

Boston Advertiser.

"Gilbert Parker writes a strong novel, but thus far this is his masterpiece. . . . It is one of the great novels of the year."

The Translation of a Savage.

Flexible cloth, 75 cents.

The Nation.

"A book which no one will be satisfied to put down until the end has been matter of certainty and assurance."

Boston Home Journal.

"A story of remarkable interest, originality, and ingenuity of construction."

London Daily News.

"The perusal of this romance will repay those who care for new and original types of character, and who are susceptible to the fascination of a fresh and vigorous style."

New York: D. APPLETON & CO., 72 Fifth Avenue.

D. APPLETON & CO.'S PUBLICATIONS.

BOOKS BY WILLIAM O. STODDARD.

CHRIS, THE MODEL-MAKER. *A Story of New York.* With 6 full-page Illustrations by B. WEST CLINEDINST. 12mo. Cloth, $1.50.

"A story like this comes home to most American youth, for it tells how a boy made his own way. It points out a path, but Mr. Stoddard is too skilled a story-teller ever to pose as a moralist, and the action of his tale moves on constantly while the interest of his pictures and incidents of New York life is unceasing."

ON THE OLD FRONTIER. With 10 full-page Illustrations. 12mo. Cloth, $1.50.

"A capital story of life in the middle of the last century. . . . The characters introduced really live and talk, and the story recommends itself not only to boys and girls but to their parents."—*New York Times.*

"An exciting narrative This tale, which relates to the last raids of the Iroquois, is as stirring as the best of those which have come from the author's pen."—*Philadelphia Evening Bulletin.*

THE BATTLE OF NEW YORK. With 11 full-page Illustrations and colored Frontispiece. 12mo. Cloth, $1.50.

"Young people who are interested in the ever thrilling story of the great rebellion will find in this romance a wonderfully graphic picture of New York in war time."—*Boston Traveler.*

"The description of these terrible days and more awful nights is very animated."—*New York Evening Post.*

LITTLE SMOKE. A story of the Sioux Indians. With 12 full-page Illustrations by F. S. DELLENBAUGH, portraits of Sitting Bull, Red Cloud, and other chiefs, and 72 head and tail pieces representing the various implements and surroundings of Indian life. 12mo. Cloth, $1.50.

"It is not only a story of adventure, but the volume abounds in information concerning this most powerful of remaining Indian tribes. The work of the author has been well supplemented by the artist."—*Boston Traveller.*

"More elaborately illustrated than any juvenile work dealing with Indian life ever published."—*Churchman.*

CROWDED OUT O' CROFIELD. The story of a country boy who fought his way to success in the great metropolis. With 23 Illustrations by C. T. HILL. 12mo. Cloth, $1.50.

"There are few writers who know how to meet the tastes and needs of boys better than does William O. Stoddard. This excellent story teaches boys to be men, not prigs or Indian hunters. If our boys would read more such books, and less of the blood-and-thunder order, it would be rare good fortune."—*Detroit Free Press.*

New York: D. APPLETON & CO., 72 Fifth Avenue.

D. APPLETON & CO.'S PUBLICATIONS.

BOOKS BY HEZEKIAH BUTTERWORTH.

THE PATRIOT SCHOOLMASTER. A Tale of the Minute Men and the Sons of Liberty. With 6 full-page Illustrations by H. WINTHROP PEIRCE. 12mo. Cloth, $1.50.

In this stirring historical romance the stately figure of Samuel Adams succeeds Lincoln and Washington in previous books as the central figures, and we live through the dramas of Boston's occupancy by the British, and Bunker Hill and Lexington. It is a story infused with noble patriotism, and most vividly told.

IN THE BOYHOOD OF LINCOLN. A Story of the Black Hawk War and the Tunker Schoolmaster. With 12 Illustrations and colored Frontispiece. 12mo. Cloth, $1.50.

"There is great fascination in these glimpses of Lincoln's early life, and the artist's accompanying pictures are very clever and welcome."—*Brooklyn Times.*

"The author presents facts in a most attractive framework of fiction, and imbues the whole with his peculiar humor. The illustrations are numerous and of more than usual excellence."—*New Haven Palladium.*

"One of the best stories for youthful readers that has ever been written."—*Boston Budget.*

"A work which should be put into the hands of every American boy."—*Philadelphia Item.*

THE BOYS OF GREENWAY COURT. A Story of the Early Years of Washington. With 10 full-page Illustrations. 12mo. Cloth, $1.50.

"Mr. Butterworth has written an excellent book, and one that young people will find delightful reading."—*Boston Beacon.*

"Skillfully combining fact and fiction, he has given us a story historically instructive and at the same time entertaining."—*Boston Transcript.*

"The book is replete with picturesque incidents and legends of hunting exploits and adventures, and the figure of young Washington is shown in a light which will be sure to enlist the interest of young readers."—*Chicago Herald.*

"Mr. Butterworth has made his story both absorbing in interest and valuable as a teacher of history."—*San Francisco Argonaut.*

THE LOG SCHOOL-HOUSE ON THE COLUMBIA. With 13 full-page Illustrations by J. CARTER BEARD, E. J. AUSTEN, and others. 12mo. Cloth, $1.50.

"This book will charm all who turn its pages. There are few books of popular information concerning the pioneers of the great Northwest, and this one is worthy of sincere praise."—*Seattle Post-Intelligencer.*

"Mr. Butterworth always interests his young readers, and holds their attention from first to last."—*New York Independent.*

New York: D. APPLETON & CO., 72 Fifth Avenue.

D. APPLETON & CO.'S PUBLICATIONS.

A JOURNEY IN OTHER WORLDS. A Romance of the Future. By JOHN JACOB ASTOR. With 9 full-page Illustrations by Dan Beard. 12mo. Cloth, $1.50.

"An interesting and cleverly devised book. . . . No lack of imagination. . . Shows a skillful and wide acquaintance with scientific facts."—*New York Herald.*

"The author speculates cleverly and daringly on the scientific advance of the earth, and he revels in the physical luxuriance of Jupiter; but he also lets his imagination travel through spiritual realms, and evidently delights in mystic speculation quite as much as in scientific investigation. If he is a follower of Jules Verne, he has not forgotten also to study the philosophers."—*New York Tribune.*

"A beautiful example of typographical art and the bookmaker's skill. . . . To appreciate the story one must read it."—*New York Commercial Advertiser.*

"The date of the events narrated in this book is supposed to be 2000 A. D. The inhabitants of North America have increased mightily in numbers and power and knowledge. It is an age of marvelous scientific attainments. Flying machines have long been in common use, and finally a new power is discovered called 'apergy,' the reverse of gravitation, by which people are able to fly off into space in any direction, and at what speed they please."—*New York Sun.*

"The scientific romance by John Jacob Astor is more than likely to secure a distinct popular success, and achieve widespread vogue both as an amusing and interesting story, and a thoughtful endeavor to prophesy some of the triumphs which science is destined to win by the year 2000. The book has been written with a purpose, and that a higher one than the mere spinning of a highly imaginative yarn. Mr. Astor has been engaged upon the book for over two years, and has brought to bear upon it a great deal of hard work in the way of scientific research, of which he has been very fond ever since he entered Harvard. It is admirably illustrated by Dan Beard."—*Mail and Express.*

"Mr. Astor has himself almost all the qualities imaginable for making the science of astronomy popular. He knows the learned maps of the astrologers. He knows the work of Copernicus. He has made calculations and observations. He is enthusiastic, and the spectacular does not frighten him."—*New York Times.*

"The work will remind the reader very much of Jules Verne in its general plan of using scientific facts and speculation as a skeleton on which to hang the romantic adventures of the central figures, who have all the daring ingenuity and luck of Mr. Verne's heroes. Mr. Astor uses history to point out what in his opinion science may be expected to accomplish. It is a romance with a purpose."—*Chicago Inter-Ocean.*

"The romance contains many new and striking developments of the possibilities of science hereafter to be explored, but the volume is intensely interesting, both as a product of imagination and an illustration of the ingenious and original application of science."—*Rochester Herald.*

New York: D. APPLETON & CO., 72 Fifth Avenue.

www.ingramcontent.com/pod-product-compliance
Lightning Source LLC
Chambersburg PA
CBHW020324240426
43673CB00039B/913